OPTICS OF COSMIC DUST
Part I

CONTENTS

Astrophys. Space Phys., 2004, Vol. 12, pp. 1–182
Reprints available directly from the publisher
Photocopying permitted by license only

OPTICS OF COSMIC DUST. PART I

N.V. Voshchinnikov

Astronomy Department and Sobolev Astronomical Institute,
St. Petersburg University, Universitetskii prosp., 28,
198504 St. Petersburg-Peterhof, Russia;
e-mail: nvv@astro.spbu.ru

ABSTRACT

The optics of small particles is useful in the interpretation of observational phenomena related to the extinction, scattering and emission of radiation by dust grains in space. Using light scattering theory for the transformation of optical constants of materials — possible cosmic dust analogues, the optical properties of grains are obtained. Further adding a model of the object one can draw comparisons with observations.

Three components of dust modelling — optical constants, light scattering theories and objects' models — are briefly discussed. The author aims to show how the general laws of the optics of dust particles work and to highlight the information about cosmic dust which is reliable and the information which can be false.

Part I of the review contains a detailed analysis of the interstellar extinction and polarization (forward-transmitted radiation).

Part II will consider the scattered radiation, dust absorption and emission, radiation pressure and dust properties in different objects.

1 WHY, WHERE AND HOW[1]

1.1 Three ways of observing dust

Dust grains have been detected in almost all astronomical objects from the local environment of the Earth to very distant galaxies and quasars. The characteristics of dust (concentration, chemical composition, size, etc.) vary significantly from one object to another even for objects of the same type. However, the following conclusion is generally valid: *interaction of radiation with grains can be described by the theory of light scattering by small particles.* This interaction includes two main processes: dust grains *scatter* and *absorb* the incident radiation. The scattered radiation with the same wavelength as the incident one propagates in different directions. The radiation absorbed by a grain is transformed into thermal energy and the particle *emits* at wavelengths usually longer than the absorbed radiation did. Both processes contribute to *extinction* when the radiation from celestial bodies is attenuated by the foreground dust in the line of sight, i.e.

$$Extinction = scattering + absorption.$$

In general, it is possible to observe the processes of *extinction*, *scattering* and *emission* of radiation by cosmic dust.

1.2 Why do astronomers study dust?

In studying cosmic dust astronomers pursue the following aims.

1. To investigate dust as an object in order to determine its properties and later to use them for understanding the general evolution of celestial objects.

2. Foreground dust disturbs the radiation of distant objects. This effect has to be well studied and its contribution must be subtracted from the observed radiation.

---

[1] The first version of the review was submitted to the Publisher in January 2002. In December 2003 the review was updated and relevant references were included.

3. When an object is mainly (or only) seen due to the presence of dust (dusty comets, reflection nebulae, infrared sources) astronomers study it through the analysis of dust. Here, infrared (IR) observations play an important role indicating the star-forming regions in our Galaxy and other galaxies.

1.3   How do astronomers study dust?

Most of the information on cosmic dust comes from the interpretation of observations of *radiation* of celestial bodies. The dusty objects are investigated in almost all regions of the electromagnetic spectrum (see Table 1). One usually observes *fluxes* which give the Spectral

Table 1 Possibilities for studying cosmic dust at different parts of the spectrum.

Wavelength range	Process[*]	Comment
γ	(none)	dust sublimation during γ-ray burst possibly could be observed as time-dependent extinction and IR emission (Waxman and Draine, 2000)
X-rays	scattering, absorption	haloes around point-like sources, absorption in K and L edges of most abundant elements
Ultraviolet	*extinction*, scattering	—
Visible	*extinction, scattering*	—
Infrared	*emission*, extinction, scattering	—
		scattering is important for the near-IR
Radio	(emission?)	possible emission of rotating grains (Draine and Lazarian, 1999)

[*] Dominant process is in italics

Energy Distribution (SED) of an object and sometimes the spatial distribution of brightness (*images* or *maps*). *Continuum* and *spectral features* (*bands*) are examined too. Exceptional information is given by observations of *polarization*. Radiation polarized by "dusty" mechanisms is found in the continuum and spectral features. The polarimetric maps of many objects (comets, nebulae, galaxies) have also been obtained.

In a few cases, it is possible to get *probes* of cosmic dust using *in situ* measurements. This may be done during missions to other planets, comets, asteroids and distant parts of the Solar System. The possibility of catching interstellar grains in flights out of the ecliptic plane is of particular interest (Grün, 1997).

Astronomers also study "celestial stones" — meteorites in which the inclusions may be considered as "old" interstellar particles processed in the Solar System.

An important role in modern investigations of cosmic dust is played by *laboratory experiments and modelling*. They include:

- measurements of the refractive indices, scattering matrices and absorption spectra of cosmic dust analogues;

- modelling of the process of refractory dust formation and growing in stellar atmospheres and protoplanetary disk environments;

- studies of molecule formation and processing of volatile dust components in conditions similar to those in dark interstellar clouds;

- experiments on grain charging and alignment.

1.4   Where is cosmic dust?

Places and *objects* where cosmic dust may be caught or observed are distributed in the order of increase of their distance from Earth:

- Earth's surface (meteorites);

- upper Earth's atmosphere (interplanetary dust and small comets);

- missions to planets, asteroids and comets (circumplanetary and cometary dust) and outside the plane of the ecliptic (interstellar dust);

- terrestrial observations of objects in the Solar System (interplanetary, circumplanetary and cometary dust, dust near the Sun);

- local interstellar medium (interstellar dust);

- general interstellar medium in our Galaxy: clouds, supernova remnants, circumstellar shells, H II regions, reflection nebulae (interstellar, circumstellar , and nebular dust);

- galaxies: normal, active, star-forming (extragalactic dust);

- very distant objects (cosmological dust).

1.5 How did the ideas on cosmic dust change?

The history of study of cosmic dust can be separated into four stages.

1.5.1 Before Trumpler

The first stage is connected with William Herschel and Wassily Struve. At that time, astronomers suspected and believed "dark holes" in the Milky Way to be the obscuring dust clouds. Considerable efforts of observers were devoted to investigations of non-luminous interstellar dust.

"Luminous" dust was discovered in 1912 when Westo Slipher found that spectra of reflection nebulae in the Pleiades were the same as those of the illuminating stars.

Near that time a Pulkovo astronomer Gavriil Tikhov first observed stars in several spectral bands. He concluded that the interstellar extinction decreased with the wavelength (Tikhov, 1910). This effect ("interstellar reddening") was included in the Master's thesis of Tikhov defended at the Petersburg University in 1912.

Note also that the interplanetary dust seen in the form of zodiacal light or cometary tails was a widely known phenomenon from ancient times.

1.5.2   *Before infrared observations (1930–60)*

The existence of dust in the interstellar medium was definitely admitted after the work of Robert Trumpler (1930) who had discovered the interstellar extinction and reddening. It reconciled contradictory points of view and explained available observational data.

The first serious model of interstellar dust was suggested by Carl Schalén (1933, 1936) who used iron particles to fit the colour excesses observed for early-type stars. Schalén approximately computed the extinction cross-sections of dust grains using Mie's (1908) scattering theory for homogeneous spheres.

Other applications of the Mie theory were made by E. Schoenberg and B. Jung (1934). They considered metallic particles and found that the observed extinction may be produced, for example, by magnesium particles. Apparently, it was the first demonstration of the *ambiguity* of dust grain models.

Bertile Lindblad (1935) suggested a progressive idea of the condensation of the meteoric matter out of the gas of interstellar clouds. It was based on the Langmuir's old experiments on the condensation of metal vapours on cold solids. This concept was taken up by Jaan Oort and Hendrik van de Hulst (1946) who found an equilibrium grain size distribution and was developed by van de Hulst in the form of a model of dielectric icy grains originating and growing in interstellar clouds. After publication of the paper of van de Hulst (1949) the model of icy grains became widely accepted and lived for many years. This classical model was modified several times by Mayo Greenberg and co-workers (Greenberg and Meltzer, 1960; Greenberg and Shah, 1966; Greenberg, 1968; Hong and Greenberg, 1980; Aannestad and Greenberg, 1983; Greenberg and Chlewicki, 1987) and is alive now in the form of the core-mantle model of Oort–van de Hulst–Greenberg (Greenberg and Li, 1996a; Li and Greenberg, 1997).

The interstellar polarization discovered in 1949 by William Hiltner (1949), John Hall (1949) and Victor Dombrovskii (1949) indicated the anisotropic nature of dust grains — most likely they are non-spherical and aligned. This very important fact caused a permanent headache for dust modellers because of the necessity to develop theories of light scattering by non-spherical particles and of alignment mechanisms. The second problem was solved rather quickly by L. Davies and J. Greenstein (1951) who suggested the mechanism of paramagnetic relaxation of dust grains in interstellar magnetic fields that is still attractive. The former problem is still not completely solved because of huge mathematical and computational difficulties[2]. Therefore, consideration of the interstellar polarization is not usually included in the modern dust models.

Polarimetric observations of various objects were performed in the 1950s–1960s at the Leningrad University (Dombrovskii), Abastumani Observatory (Vashakidze), Observatory of Haut Provence (Martel), Lowell Observatory and University of Arizona (Elvius, Hall, Coyne, Gehrels, Serkowski), Alma-Ata Observatory (Rozhkovskii), Stockholm Observatory (Behr), Crimean Observatory (Shakhovskoi), McDonald Observatory (Hiltner), Burakan Observatory (Grigorian and Khachikian). The observations were made at several wavelengths for early and late-type stars, diffuse and reflection nebulae, supernova remnants, galaxies. In almost all cases, the mechanisms of polarization were found to be extinction and scattering by dust grains. More complicated cases of variable circumstellar polarization were discovered as well.

Investigations of circumstellar shells roused Fred Hoyle and Nalin Wickramasinghe (1962) to consider the atmospheres of cool carbon stars as a source of graphite grains. They developed a harmonious theory of nucleation and growth of grains in stellar atmospheres and their subsequent ejection into the interstellar medium by the radiation pressure. In interstellar clouds bare particles may accumulate icy mantles from volatile elements which should lead to the core-mantle grains. The optical properties of such particles were first studied by Wickramasinghe (1963).

---

[2] For the simplest model of non-spherical particles — infinite circular cylinders — the calculations can easily be performed but it is not physically reasonable and may be used only for rough estimates.

Thus, at this stage investigations of cosmic dust had been started, however, many astronomers were considering dust *as an obstacle*. This was the case untill the appearance of IR observations.

1.5.3   Infrared observations and laboratory astrophysics (1970–90)

Infrared astronomy is the field where the study of warm dust emission dominates. The first IR observations of late-type stars were performed by N. Woolf and E. Ney (1969). They showed that the observed fluxes exceeded by several times the predicted ones from the theory of stellar atmospheres. After the first IR sky reviews [IRC (1969), AFGL (1975) and especially those made at the *Infrared Astronomical Satellite* (IRAS, 1984)], it was established that *almost all cosmic objects from the interplanetary medium to galaxies are IR sources*. The common reason for their emission is radiation of dust grains heated by the ambient radiation field. However, in hot shocked gas, heating of dust by shock waves occurs as well.

Besides continuum radiation, IR astronomy studies vibrational transitions in cosmic solids that gives the possibility of examining the chemical composition of dust grains (especially in dense clouds). The most famous IR feature is "silicate" band observed in emission or absorption near $\lambda 9.7\,\mu m$ in various objects and attributed to the stretching transition in the Si–O bond. Unfortunately, an unambiguous identification of the constituent (material) is impossible. The search for new transitions to be observed was the reason for many laboratory investigations. They initiated studies the processing and chemical evolution of volatile components of dust grains which are frozen on cold surfaces and then irradiated by protons and UV photons, heated, evaporated and refrozen again, etc. The investigations were and are very important for understanding of processes of interstellar molecule formation and desorption and grain mantle growth.

Another way to study the composition of interstellar dust was opened in the 1970s by the possibility of observing the UV lines due to interstellar gas absorption lines. The observations made at the Orbiting Astronomical Observatory (OAO) "Copernicus" showed that the gas-phase abundances of many elements are smaller than the corresponding solar abundances. The residual amount of the elements was attributed to be locked in the dust component of the interstel-

lar medium. This idea was supported by the observational fact that
the depletions are smaller in high velocity interstellar clouds where
the dust grains should be partly destroyed. New observational data
from OAO "Copernicus" inspired J. Mathis, W. Rumpl and K. Nordsieck (1977) to create the first contemporary silicate-graphite model
of interstellar grains (MRN mixture). By fitting the interstellar extinction curve from UV to near IR region Mathis *et al.* deduced
a power law size distribution for a two component model. Later,
B. Draine and H. Lee (1984) modified the MRN model on the basis
of carefully selected optical constants. Mathis (1986) also attempted
to include the polarization in this model: he considered the cylindrical silicate grains while the graphite particles were assumed to be
spheres. Mathis and Whiffen (1989) modified the MRN model by
introduction of composite grains which are aggregates of small amorphous carbon, silicate and iron particles. The optical properties of
composite particles were calculated with Mie theory and the Effective Medium Theory which was used preliminarily to find the optical
constants.

1.5.4   *ISO revolution and carbon crisis (last decade of XXth century)*

In this period, new important observational data on cosmic dust were
obtained from the *Infrared Space Observatory* (ISO), *Hubble Space
Telescope* (HST), *COsmic Background Explorer* (COBE). During the
ISO space mission new features of many solid species including various ices, sulfides, crystalline silicates have been discovered. Along
with the detection of many molecules in the gas phase, this was named
by the *ISO Revolution* (d'Hendecourt *et al.*, 1999). The unexpected
detection of crystalline silicates around young and evolved stars and
in comets initiated the origin of *astromineralogy* — a new branch of
astronomy (Molster, 2000; Henning, 2003a).

Observations of the UV absorption lines with the HST (Savage
and Sembach, 1996) gave interstellar gas-phase abundances in many
directions. Spectroscopic study of ordinary stars allowed one to de-
duce new cosmic abundances of heavy elements which were, apparently, 60–70% of the solar abundances (Snow and Witt, 1996). These
data limited the number of atoms incorporated into dust particles.

The most critical situation occurred for carbon which is the main component of many dust models. The inability to explain the observed extinction using the amount of carbon available in the solid phase resulted in so called "*carbon crisis*" which has not been resolved up to now.

Observations of the interstellar polarization in the far-UV were performed on the HST and during the Wisconsin Ultraviolet Photo Polarimeter Experiment. They show an unpredictable behaviour of polarization near the UV extinction bump (Martin *et al.*, 1999) which is still not interpreted.

Study of the cosmic IR background radiation with COBE led to the development of detailed models of the dust distribution in the zodiacal cloud (Wright, 1998; Gojian *et al.*, 2000) and in the interstellar medium (Arendt *et al.*, 1998).

More historical facts related to the development of dusty astrophysics can be found in a comprehensive review of Dorschner (2003).

1.6   Where does dust come from and how does it evolve?

Formation and evolution of dust grains in the interstellar medium includes several stages.

- *formation* of refractory grains in the atmospheres of late-type stars

   This is the primary mechanism of the replenishment of dust in the Galaxy. Solid particles originate from homogeneous or heterogeneous nucleation in the expanding atmospheres of luminous red giants which have reached an Asymptotic Giant Branch (AGB). A small contribution to the total amount of galactic dust comes from novae, supergiants and the Wolf–Rayet stars of types WC8 and WC9.

   The chemical composition of forming dust is determined by the ratio C/O in the stellar atmosphere. Oxygen-rich stars (M-type giants) produce Mg–Fe silicates and various oxides, mainly in the form of amorphous compounds. In the envelopes of C-type giants, disordered carbon, silicon carbide and sulfides should form.

- *formation* in supernovae

  Possibly, some amount of interstellar particles form in the ejects of Type II supernovae[3]. The composition of such grains is expected to be rather exotic and they may be responsible for the isotopic anomalies detected in meteorites.

- *growth* in the atmospheres of late-type stars

  Small particles formed in the winds of AGB stars move outward under the action of radiation pressure. They grow due to the processes of condensation and deposition of gaseous species and, possibly, coagulation (in grain–grain collisions). So, the stardust grains fetched up in the interstellar medium may already possess rather a complicated structure with voids, inclusions and mantles.

- *growth and processing* in interstellar clouds

  Inside interstellar clouds, especially dense ones, dust grains grow by accretion of volatile species from the gas phase and by coagulation. Both processes lead to the formation of inhomogeneous grains, although coagulation should also produce porous particles and aggregates and modify the grain size distribution. Icy mantles are irradiated by UV photons and energetic ions, chemically evolve and may result in the appearance of multilayered grains.

- *destruction* in interstellar shocks

  The shock waves from supernova explosions or energetic stellar winds destroy dust grains by sputtering. Grain–grain collisions provoked by the passage of a shock wave cause shattering of particles and change their initial size distribution.

- *destruction* in star-forming regions

  Part of the dust grains in dense interstellar clouds may be involved in the process of star formation and broken down. At

---

[3] Observations of supernova remnants Cas A (Dunne *et al.*, 2003) and Kepler (Morgan *et al.*, 2003) at submillimeter wavelengths showed the presence of cold dust. The total mass of dust implied is $\sim 1 M_\odot$ for Kepler and $\sim 2 - 4 M_\odot$ for Cas A which is about 10^3 times greater than previous estimates (see, however, discussion in Dwek (2004)).

the same time, a fraction of grains continues to live and evolve around a star for a long time and appears later in the form of an interplanetary dust cloud or as constituents of cometary nuclei.

Different types of dust populations and their evolutionary relationship are shown in Fig. 1. Paradoxically that *dust around old stars is young* whereas *dust around young stars is old.*

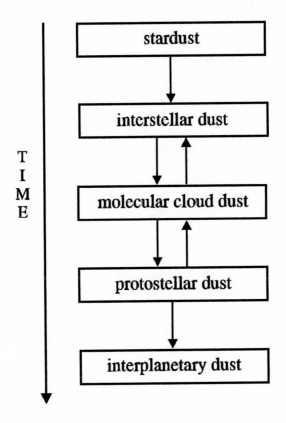

Figure 1 The dust populations. After Henning (1999).

The discussion of the metamorphoses of solid particles in the circumstellar envelopes, the diffuse interstellar medium, molecular clouds, protoplanetary environments can be found in the reviews of Dorschner and Henning (1995) and Henning (1999) and the book by Whittet (2003). Draine (2003a, 2003b) considers various observational and theoretical aspects of investigations of interstellar dust grains. Excellent introduction to the physics of cosmic dust is given by Krügel (2003).

1.7 Three components of dust modelling

Before one starts creating a model, we need to consider the common features of the observational phenomena. The model must describe these features. Some possibilities of investigating the cosmic dust are given in Table 2. Usually, the models are mainly assigned to fit the interstellar extinction.

Interpretation of observations of dusty objects can be divided into three steps. By analogy with cooking a delicate dish, the "*kitchen of dust modelling*" includes:

1. laying-in *provision*

   The primary task is to find elements which can be converted into the solid state in the circumstellar/interstellar conditions and to determine the resulting *materials*. There is an important condition: *the element abundance must not exceed that in the solid state* which is the difference between the cosmic and gaseous abundances.

   The next task is to measure or to find the *optical constants* (refractive indices) of the materials under consideration.

   Mixing the optical constants is often made to simulate the properties of composite grains.

2. choice of *equipment*

   Selection of *light scattering theory* ("equipment") is an essential aspect in dust modelling. An improper choice of the tool may result in the spoiling of provision. Note that the chosen method

Table 2 Possibilities for studying cosmic dust in different objects.

Object	Extinction and polarization in the line of sight[*]	Scattered radiation	Continuum IR radiation	IR features
Diffuse clouds	+	0	+	0
Molecular clouds	+	0	+	+
Cirrus	0	+	+	−
Globules	+	0	+	0
Reflection nebulae	0	+	0	0
Planetary and diffuse nebulae	0	0	+	+
Circumstellar shells	0	+	+	+
Zodiacal dust[**]	−	+	+.	0
Cometary dust	0	+	+	+
Dust in other galaxies	+	0	+	+

[*] Interstellar extinction and polarization for galactic clouds; [**] Orbital motion of the zodiacal dust particles may be observed in the form of Doppler shifts of the Fraunhofer lines in the zodiacal light (see discussion in Mann, 1998); "+" — effective method; "0" — possible, but rarely used method; "−" — observations are impossible or are not carried out.

has to give the possibility to represent the most significant features of the observational phenomenon and to work rather fast in order to give results in a reasonable time.

3. *cooking*

This most important part of the procedure is related to the skill of the cook (modeller) and includes not only a selection of provision and equipment but also a proper choice of the method of cooking — *object modelling.* Wrongly treated a model easily disarranges the carefully prepared things.

Lastly, one needs to taste the prepared dish, i.e. to compare the model with observations. The latter are performed with a limited accuracy which imposes the corresponding claim on the model. From other side, a very complicated and detailed model with many parameters is ambiguous in principle. Complicating the model, one should not forget about the principle of optical equivalence introduced by George Gabriel Stokes 150 years ago:

It is impossible to distinguish two beams which are the sum of non-coherent simple waves if they have the same Stokes parameters.

So, a judicious restriction on the detailed elaboration of different components in dust modelling should be found.

1.8   New observations versus old theories

Modern astronomical technique develops so swiftly that the theory cannot keep up with it. A permanent delay of the theoretical models relative to new observational data results in an ignorance of part of the observational information.

Nowadays, observations provide us information on many details of objects structure and spectra BUT still:

i) there is no dust model explaining the observed interstellar extinction and cosmic abundances together;

ii) a grain model which explains the interstellar polarization observed in a wide spectral range is absent;

iii) mechanisms of formation and the growth of non-spherical grains are not yet developed in detail;

iv) ... *et cetera.*

Apparently, it is naive to think that a unified model of cosmic dust will be created (at least soon). The conditions and the evolutionary history of different parts of the Galaxy are different to such an extent that dust there cannot even be similar. However, some vital blocks of model based on the general laws and observations can be built.

It is the aim of this review to show how the general laws of *optics of dust particles* work and what information about the cosmic dust is reliable, what may be dubious and what is false.

2   KITCHEN OF DUST MODELLING

2.1   Provision

2.1.1   Abundances and depletions

The abundances of elements in the interstellar medium are determined as the number of atoms relative to that of hydrogen, $[X/H]$, where X (or N_X) and H (or $N_H = N_{HI} + 2N_{H_2}$) are the column densities of an element X and hydrogen in a given direction. The abundances by number are usually expressed as the number of X atoms per 10^6 hydrogen nuclei (parts per million, ppm, hereafter).

Ultraviolet and optical absorption-line studies have shown that the interstellar (gas-phase) abundances of many elements are lower than cosmic (reference) abundances. The rest of elements is assumed to be embedded in solid particles. The depletion of an element X is defined by

$$D_X = \left[\frac{X}{H}\right]_g \Bigg/ \left[\frac{X}{H}\right]_{cosmic} . \qquad (2.1)$$

The logarithmic quantities

$$\delta_X = \log D_X = \log \left[\frac{X}{H}\right]_g - \log \left[\frac{X}{H}\right]_{cosmic} \qquad (2.2)$$

are also used.

Traditionally, the cosmic (reference) abundances are assumed to be equal to the solar ones (or more exactly, to the Solar System abundances which are obtained from solar photospheric and meteoritic abundance determinations). The reference abundances are compared with those measured in different galactic and extragalactic objects despite the fact that the solar abundances reflect the chemical composition of a star (Sun) of given age at given distance from the galactic centre. Temporal and spatial abundance trends of abundances in the Galaxy are a subject of growing number of observational and theoretical investigations (see, e.g., Alibés *et al.*, 2001 and discussion in Sect. 3.2.4). At the same time, the photospheric abundances of the Sun are a matter of permanent study, revision and update. The most widely used solar abundances were compiled by Anders

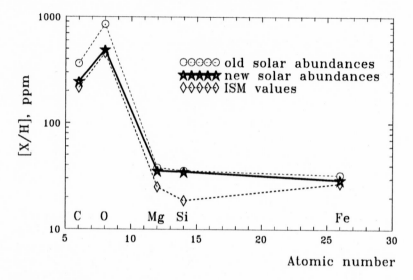

Figure 2 Abundances of five elements forming cosmic grains. The data for old and new solar abundances were taken from Anders and Grevesse (1989) and Lodders (2003), respectively. Stellar abundances are according to Snow and Witt (1996).

and Grevesse (1989). From the abundances of cluster and field B stars, and young F, G stars, Snow and Witt (1996) found that many species in these stars were significantly underabundant (by a factor of 1.5–2.0) relative to the data given by Anders and Grevesse. This circumstance caused the discomfort conditions for the modelling of the observed interstellar extinction and was often ignored (see discussion in Sect. 3.2.5). However, during the past several years the solar abundances dropped and now they approach to the stellar ones. Lodders (2003) summarized the elemental abundances in the solar photosphere derived from spectroscopy and CI chondrites. The values recommended by her will be referred to as "new reference abundances". The old and new solar abundances as well as the stellar abundances according to Snow and Witt (1996) are given in Fig. 2 and Table 3 for five main elements forming cosmic dust grains.

Table 3 Solar and stellar abundances of five elements forming cosmic dust (in ppm)

Element	old solar [1]	new solar [2]	stellar [3]	$\left[\frac{X}{H}\right]_d$ for ζ Oph
C	363	245	214	110
O	851	490	457	159
Mg	38.0	35.4	25	33.4
Si	35.5	34.7	18.6	33.1
Fe	32.4	29.1	27	29.1

[1] Anders and Grevesse (1989); [2] Lodders (2003); [3] Snow and Witt (1996). Fifth column gives the dust-phase abundances in the line of sight to the star ζ Oph. They were calculated as a difference between new solar abundances and gas phase abundances in this direction from Snow and Witt (1996; the abundance of Mg was recalculated with the new oscillator forces from Fitzpatrick, 1997).

A.P. Jones (2000) divided potential dust-forming elements into four groups. Carbon and oxygen are the *primary* dust constituents, while Mg, Si and Fe the *major* dust constituents. Also there are *minor* dust constituents (Na, Al, Ca and Ni, dust-phase abundance $\lesssim 3$ ppm) and *trace* dust constituents (K, Ti, Cr, Mn and Co, dust-phase abundance $\lesssim 0.3$ ppm).

The dust-phase abundances can be found as

$$\left[\frac{X}{H}\right]_d = \left[\frac{X}{H}\right]_{cosmic} - \left[\frac{X}{H}\right]_g = \left[\frac{X}{H}\right]_{cosmic} (1 - D_X). \qquad (2.3)$$

In Table 3, the dust abundances are given for the star ζ Oph using the new system of reference abundances. Although the validity of this system is under discussion (see Sofia and Meyer, 2001; Draine, 2003a), it shook all existing grain models because the observed interstellar extinction must be explained with a significantly reduced amount of material in the solid phase. The major problem is to satisfy the carbon abundances, e.g., for ζ Oph, $\delta_C = -0.43$ and -0.26 in old and new reference systems, respectively. This means that the abundance $[C/H]_d$ reduced from 228 ppm to 110 ppm.

Note also that the dust-phase abundances vary strongly in different directions. For example, in the direction of star ξ Per carbon is almost undepleted in the new reference system (see Table 7 in Savage and Sembach, 1996), even though the extinction curve for this star shows the pronounced UV bump (Fitzpatrick and Massa, 1990) which is usually attributed to graphite particles. For local interstellar medium (ISM), the dust abundances of Mg (18 ppm), Si (7 ppm) and Fe (24 ppm) are smaller than the corresponding abundances in the direction of ζ Oph (Frisch *et al.*, 1999).

2.1.2   Optical constants

The complex refractive indices or *dielectric functions* of solids are called *optical constants* but in reality they are not constant but the *wavelength-dependent* quantities. They appear when the Maxwell equations are supplemented with the material equations

$$\vec{D} = \varepsilon\vec{E}, \quad \vec{B} = \mu\vec{H}, \quad \vec{j} = \sigma\vec{E}. \tag{2.4}$$

Here, $\vec{E}$ and $\vec{H}$ are the vectors of the electric and magnetic fields, $\vec{D}$ is the dielectric displacement, $\vec{B}$ the magnetic flux density, $\vec{j}$ the current density, ε and μ are the dielectric permittivity and the magnetic permeability of a medium, σ is the conductivity. Media are often assumed to be isotropic, homogeneous and linear, which means the independence of ε, μ and σ on direction, coordinates and fields, respectively.

For harmonically variable fields ($\vec{E}, \vec{H} \propto e^{-i\omega t}$, $\omega = 2\pi\nu = 2\pi c/\lambda$ – the circular frequency, c – the speed of light), the Maxwell equations are transformed to the Helmholtz (wave) equations

$$\nabla^2\vec{E} + k^2\vec{E} = 0, \quad \nabla^2\vec{H} + k^2\vec{H} = 0, \tag{2.5}$$

with the complex wave-number

$$k = k_0 m = \frac{\omega}{c}\sqrt{\mu\left(\varepsilon + i\frac{4\pi\sigma}{\omega}\right)}. \tag{2.6}$$

Here, $k_0 = \omega/c = 2\pi/\lambda$ is the wave-number in free space (vacuum). The complex refractive index

$$m = \sqrt{\mu\left(\varepsilon + i\frac{4\pi\sigma}{\omega}\right)} \tag{2.7}$$

is of great importance in the optics of scattering media. It is an initial product for further processing and it is necessary to know how it is measured and how qualitative it is.

The refractive index is written in the form $m = n(1 + \varkappa i)$ or $m = n + ki$, where $k = n\varkappa \geq 0$. The sign of the imaginary part of the refractive index is opposite to that of the time-dependent multiplier in the presentation of fields[4].

The physical sense of n and k becomes clear if one considers the solution to the wave equations (2.5) in an absorbing medium. For an electric field propagating, for example, in the z-direction, we have

$$\vec{E} = \vec{E}_0 \exp\left(-\frac{\omega}{c}kz\right) \exp\left[-i\omega\left(t - \frac{nz}{c}\right)\right]. \qquad (2.8)$$

As it is seen from Eq. (2.8), the imaginary part k (often named the extinction coefficient or index) characterizes damping or absorption of the wave. The real part n (the refraction index) determines the phase velocity of the wave in the medium, $v_{\text{phase}} = c/n$.

The travelling-wave solution (2.8) can be rewritten using the dielectric function

$$\varepsilon = \varepsilon' + \varepsilon'' i. \qquad (2.9)$$

The relation between m and ε can be found from Eq. (2.7)

$$\varepsilon' = n^2 - k^2, \qquad \varepsilon'' = 2nk - \frac{4\pi\sigma}{\omega} \qquad (2.10)$$

and

$$n = \left[\frac{\sqrt{(\varepsilon')^2 + (\varepsilon'' + \frac{4\pi\sigma}{\omega})^2} + \varepsilon'}{2}\right]^{1/2},$$

$$k = \left[\frac{\sqrt{(\varepsilon')^2 + (\varepsilon'' + \frac{4\pi\sigma}{\omega})^2} - \varepsilon'}{2}\right]^{1/2}. \qquad (2.11)$$

Here we assume $\mu = 1$, which is valid for all non-ferromagnetic materials.

---

[4] Note that in the book of van de Hulst (1957) the refractive index is chosen as $m = n - ki$ whereas in the book of Bohren and Huffman (1983) as $m = n + ki$.

There are two types of media of interest. The first one is a dielectric, or a poor conductor, for which $4\pi\sigma/\omega \ll 1$ and then $m = \sqrt{\varepsilon}$. In a material with high conductivity such as metals in the infrared, however, $4\pi\sigma/\omega \gg 1$ and

$$n \simeq k \simeq \sqrt{\frac{2\pi\sigma}{\omega}}. \tag{2.12}$$

For measurements of the optical constants, superpositions of the transmittance and reflection methods are used. The values of k may be found from measurement of absorption in a layer of thickness L: $I = I_0 \exp[-(4\pi k/\lambda)L]$, where I and I_0 are the intensities of transmitted and incident light. The values of n are obtained from measurements of the coefficient of reflection from the plane layer $\mathcal{R}$ utilizing the Fresnel formulae (Shifrin, 1951)

$$n = \frac{1+\mathcal{R}}{1-\mathcal{R}} + \sqrt{\left(\frac{1+\mathcal{R}}{1-\mathcal{R}}\right)^2 - 1 - k^2} \simeq 1 + 2\mathcal{R} + \sqrt{4\mathcal{R} - k^2}. \tag{2.13}$$

The last approximate expression is obtained if $\mathcal{R} \ll 1$.

For non-transparent materials, one tries to measure the coefficient $\mathcal{R}$ in a wide wavelength range and then applies the Kramers–Kronig relations. These general integral dispersion relations demonstrate that the real and imaginary parts of the optical constants are not independent and may be calculated one from another. When applied to n and k, the relations are

$$n(\omega) = 1 + \frac{2}{\pi}\mathcal{P}\int_0^\infty \frac{\Omega k(\Omega)}{\Omega^2 - \omega^2}\, d\Omega, \tag{2.14}$$

$$k(\omega) = -\frac{2\omega}{\pi}\mathcal{P}\int_0^\infty \frac{n(\Omega)}{\Omega^2 - \omega^2}\, d\Omega, \tag{2.15}$$

where $\mathcal{P}$ denotes the principal part of the integral.

Equations (2.14) and (2.15) allow one to make some conclusions on the behaviour of the optical constants in different wavelength ranges. In particular, it is impossible to have a material with $k = 0$ at all wavelengths because in this case the radiation does not interact with the material ($n = 1$).

The absorption features are *footprints* of a given material which help to identify the chemical composition of the solid particles (see Part II, Sect. 7 for details). In the IR (small frequencies), vibration of lattice dominates, while in the UV (large frequencies) excitation of intrinsic vibrations of electrons occurs. For very high frequencies (in X-ray region), all types of vibrations disappear as follows from Eq. (2.14)

$$\lim_{\omega \to \infty} n(\omega) = 1.$$

This is the *general* behaviour of any material.

Note also that although for very large wavelengths the asymptotic behaviour of the real part of the refractive index n is determined by the absorption as a whole, the major contribution is due to the absorption at low frequencies. This follows from Eq. (2.14) for $\omega = 0$

$$n(0) = 1 + \frac{2}{\pi} \int_0^\infty \frac{k(\Omega)}{\Omega} \, d\Omega. \tag{2.16}$$

Figure 3 illustrates the wavelength dependence of the refractive indices of two types of materials: with metallic (iron, amorphous carbon) and dielectric (ice, astronomical silicate) properties.   It is seen that the difference in the optical constants is significant for different materials. Although these constants cannot usually be applied directly to interpretation of observations without the process of "cultivation" by means of light scattering theory, the following rule is generally correct: *A feature of dust arises in the spectrum of an object if the bond is present in the optical constants of materials.*

The optical constants for amorphous carbon and astronomical silicate plotted in Fig. 4 allow one to understand the relation between the real and imaginary parts of the refractive indices better. In particular, the limiting and asymptotic values of n and k are clearly seen. Note that the absorption features appear as loops in the $k - n$ diagrams.

2.1.3   WWW database of optical constants

Physical conditions in cosmic objects require one to know the optical constants in a wide spectral range measured at different temperatures.

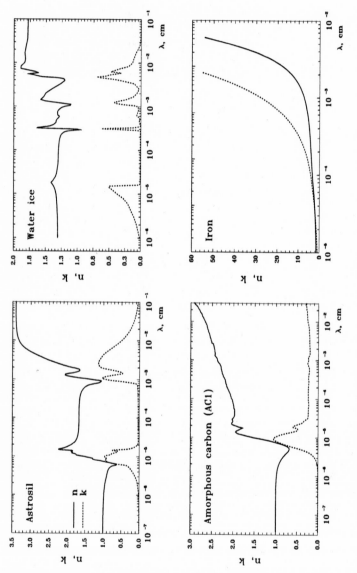

Figure 3 Wavelength dependence of the refractive indices of four materials. The sources of the optical constants are given in Table 4. For water ice, the value of k was chosen to be equal 0.01 in the range $\lambda = 0.17$–2.7 μm.

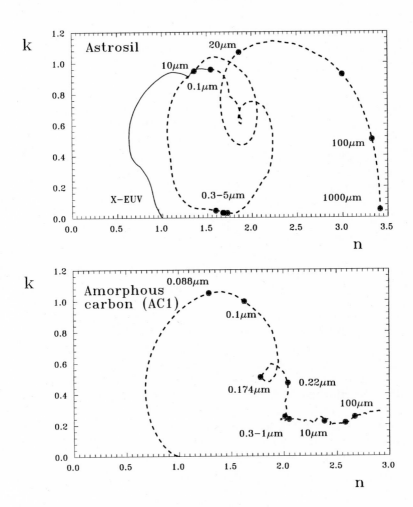

Figure 4 Refractive indices of two materials. The values of wavelengths given in μm are indicated.

Up to now astronomers have used the optical constants of natural minerals measured in the laboratory. Sometimes, the artificial materials like "astronomical silicate" (astrosil; Draine and Lee, 1984) or dirty OHM-silicate (Ossenkopf *et al.*, 1992) were employed. In these cases, the laboratory data together with observed profiles of IR features and Kramers–Kronig analysis were applied to find the refractive indices. Note that because the optical constants are macroscopic quantities, they lose their sense for molecules and clusters of molecules. In visible and near-IR, the size-dependent effects in the refractive indices appear for small clusters of some metals like silver (which is unimportant for astronomical applications) but they seem to be neglected for pure iron (Kreibig and Vollmer, 1995). However, small-particle effects are expected to occur for graphite particles radii r_s comparable to or smaller than the mean free path for electrons or holes in the bulk material. According to Draine and Lee (1984), the dielectric function $\varepsilon_\perp$ for the case of orientation of the electric field perpendicular to the basal plane of graphite are expected to be appreciably modified in the IR. The effect manifests itself for particles with radii smaller than the critical one: $r_s\,[\mu\mathrm{m}] \leq r_{s,\mathrm{crit}} = 1.9/(1 + 0.322 T_d + 0.0013 T_d^2)$, where T_d is the dust temperature. For $T_d = 20$ K, the difference in values of $\varepsilon_\perp$ for particles of different radii becomes noticeable if $\lambda \gtrsim 5\,\mu\mathrm{m}$ (Draine, 1985).

However, in the last few years special measurements of the optical constants for cosmic dust analogues were executed (see Ehrenfreund, 1999; Henning and Mutschke, 2000 and Henning, 2003b for a review). A very large amount of work in this direction was performed in the laboratory of Astrophysical Institute of Friedrich Schiller University (Jena, Germany) and in the Leiden Molecular Astrophysics Group (The Netherlands). The Jena's data as well as the data derived in the Soviet Union and some often used freely accessible data were the foundation of the database of optical constants for astronomy (Jena–Petersburg Database of Optical Constants, JPDOC; see Henning *et al.*, 1999; Jäger *et al.*, 2003). It contains references to the papers, data files and links to the Internet resources related to measurements and calculations of the optical constants of materials of astronomical interest in the wavelength interval from X-rays to the radio domain. The groups of materials are:

- silicates: amorphous, glassy, crystalline;

- silicon and silicon oxides: silicon, crystalline and fused quartz, etc.;

- metals: iron, magnesium and others;

- oxides: (Fe/Mg) oxides, hematite, magnetite, corundum, spinel, etc.;

- sulfides: (Fe/Mg) sulfides, SiS_2;

- carbides: SiC, FeC, TiC;

- carbonaceous species: amorphous and glassy carbon, coals, kerogen, graphite, diamonds, etc.;

- organics: tholin, "organic refractory";

- ices: water ice, CO/CO_2 ice, ammonia ice, other ices, ice mixtures;

- space materials: lunar, planetary, meteoritic, etc.

Examples of the refractive indices of materials of different groups are given in Table 4.

The database has free access via the Internet (see the address in Sect. 5.2).

2.1.4 Mixing the optical constants (Effective Medium Theory)

The conditions in which cosmic dust grains originate and grow should lead to the formation of heterogeneous particles with complicated structure. The problem of electromagnetic radiation scattering by such composite particles is so difficult that its solution is practically impossible, in particular keeping in mind the unknown real structure of grains.

Therefore, it is very attractive to have a way to get the optical properties of heterogeneous particles using homogeneous particles with *averaged* or *effective* dielectric functions ε_{eff} found from a

Table 4 The refractive indices for cosmic dust analog materials at $\lambda = 0.55\,\mu$m.

Group: material	$m = n + ki$	Reference
silicates:		
glassy pyroxene: $Mg_{0.5}Fe_{0.5}SiO_3$	$1.61 + 1.65 \cdot 10^{-3}i$	[1]
glassy olivine: $MgFeSiO_4$	$1.758 + 8.44 \cdot 10^{-2}i$	[1]
silicon and silicon oxides:		
silicon: Si	$4.07 + 2.84 \cdot 10^{-2}i$	[2]
quartz: α-SiO_2	$1.546 + 0.0i$	[3]
metals: Fe	$2.59 + 3.62i$	[4]
oxides: FeO	$2.380 + 0.6897i$	[5]
MgO	$1.741 + 6.55 \cdot 10^{-7}i$	[6]
sulfides: FeS_2	$2.60 + 3.12i$	[7]
carbides: SiC	$2.52 + 0.908 \cdot 10^{-3}i$	[8]
carbonaceous species:		
amorphous carbon: AC1	$1.98 + 0.232i$	[9]
organics: organic refractory	$1.953 + 0.290i$	[10]
ices: water ice	$1.306 + 3.11 \cdot 10^{-9}i$	[11]
space materials: astrosil	$1.679 + 0.030i$	[8]

[1] Dorschner *et al.* (1995); [2] Geist (1998); [3] Philipp (1985), ordinary ray; [4] Leksina and Penkina (1967); [5] Henning *et al.* (1995); [6] Roessler and Huffman (1991); [7] Palik (1998); [8] Laor and Draine (1993); [9] Rouleau and Martin (1991); [10] Greenberg and Li (1996b); [11] Warren (1984), for dirty ice $k = 0.01$ was taken.

mixing rule (generally called the Effective Medium Theory; EMT). Mathematically, this corresponds to the equation

$$\int_V \vec{D}(x,y,z)\,\mathrm{d}x\,\mathrm{d}y\,\mathrm{d}z = \int_V \varepsilon(x,y,z)\vec{E}(x,y,z)\,\mathrm{d}x\,\mathrm{d}y\,\mathrm{d}z$$

$$= \varepsilon_{\text{eff}} \int_V \vec{E}(x,y,z)\,\mathrm{d}x\,\mathrm{d}y\,\mathrm{d}z, \qquad (2.17)$$

where the inhomogeneity of a particle is introduced by the dependence of the dielectric permittivity on the position $\varepsilon(x,y,z)$.

The EMTs for mixtures are traditionally considered in the framework of electrostatic fields (Sihvola, 1999). This means that spatial variations of the electric field have to be weaker than variations in the structure of the medium. So, the sizes of inhomogeneities in a matrix or the correlation distance (in the case of a medium being described by the a continuous permittivity function) has to be considerably smaller than the wavelength of electromagnetic radiation in the medium (host material) $\lambda_{medium} = \lambda_{vacuum}/m_{medium}$. Also, the shape and orientation of inclusions as well as their volume fraction may vary.

There are many different mixing rules (see Petrov, 1986; Sihvola, 1999 and Chýlek *et al.*, 2000 for a review). They are rediscovered from time to time and can occasionally be obtained one from another. The most popular EMTs are the classical mixing rules of (Maxwell) Garnett (1904) and Bruggeman (1935). In the case of spherical inclusions and a two-component medium the effective dielectric constant may easily be calculated from the dielectric permittivities ε_1, ε_2 and volume fractions f, $1 - f$ of the components (see Table 5). The Garnett rule assumes that one material is a matrix (host material) in which the other material is embedded. When the roles of the inclusion and the host material are reversed, the inverse Garnett rule is obtained. The Bruggeman rule is symmetric with respect to the interchange of materials.

Sihvola (1989) suggested a general formula for several mixing rules

$$\frac{\varepsilon_{eff} - \varepsilon_2}{\varepsilon_{eff} + 2\varepsilon_2 + \tilde{\nu}(\varepsilon_{eff} - \varepsilon_2)} = f\frac{\varepsilon_1 - \varepsilon_2}{\varepsilon_1 + 2\varepsilon_2 + \tilde{\nu}(\varepsilon_{eff} - \varepsilon_2)}, \qquad (2.18)$$

where $\tilde{\nu}$ is an arbitrary positive number. Equation (2.18) gives the Garnett rule if $\tilde{\nu} = 0$, the Böttcher and Bruggeman formulae if $\tilde{\nu} = 2$ and the quasi-crystalline approximation if $\tilde{\nu} = 3$.

The power-law models of Looyenga and Birchak (Table 5) can be written in the common form (Kärkkäinen *et al.*, 1999)

$$\varepsilon_{eff}^{\tilde{\beta}} = f\varepsilon_1^{\tilde{\beta}} + (1 - f)\varepsilon_2^{\tilde{\beta}}, \qquad (2.19)$$

where $\tilde{\beta}$ is a dimensionless parameter. The rules of Birchak and Looyenga are derived if $\tilde{\beta} = 1/2$ and $\tilde{\beta} = 1/3$, respectively.

Table 5 Mixing rules for the refractive indices.

N	Mixing rule	$m_{\text{eff}} = n + ki^{(*)}$
1	Garnett (1904): $$\varepsilon_{\text{eff}} = \varepsilon_2 \left[1 + \frac{3f\frac{\varepsilon_1 - \varepsilon_2}{\varepsilon_1 + 2\varepsilon_2}}{1 - f\frac{\varepsilon_1 - \varepsilon_2}{\varepsilon_1 + 2\varepsilon_2}} \right]$$	$1.516 + 0.021i$
2	Inverse Garnett: $$\varepsilon_{\text{eff}} = \varepsilon_1 \left[1 + \frac{3(1 - f)\frac{\varepsilon_2 - \varepsilon_1}{\varepsilon_2 + 2\varepsilon_1}}{1 - (1 - f)\frac{\varepsilon_2 - \varepsilon_1}{\varepsilon_2 + 2\varepsilon_1}} \right]$$	—
3	Bruggeman (1935): $$f\frac{\varepsilon_1 - \varepsilon_{\text{eff}}}{\varepsilon_1 + 2\varepsilon_{\text{eff}}} + (1 - f)\frac{\varepsilon_2 - \varepsilon_{\text{eff}}}{\varepsilon_2 + 2\varepsilon_{\text{eff}}} = 0$$	$1.539 + 0.024i$
4	Böttcher (1952): $$\frac{\varepsilon_{\text{eff}} - \varepsilon_2}{3\varepsilon_{\text{eff}}} = f\frac{\varepsilon_1 - \varepsilon_2}{\varepsilon_1 + 2\varepsilon_{\text{eff}}}$$	$1.539 + 0.024i$
5	Quasi-crystalline approximation (Tsang *et al.*, 1985): $$\varepsilon_{\text{eff}} = \varepsilon_2 + f(\varepsilon_1 - \varepsilon_2)\frac{3\varepsilon_{\text{eff}}}{3\varepsilon_{\text{eff}} + (1 - f)(\varepsilon_1 - \varepsilon_2)}$$	$1.582 + 0.026i$
6	Looyenga (1965): $$\varepsilon_{\text{eff}}^{1/3} = f\varepsilon_1^{1/3} + (1 - f)\varepsilon_2^{1/3}$$	$1.534 + 0.023i$
7	Birchak (Birchak *et al.*, 1974): $$\varepsilon_{\text{eff}}^{1/2} = f\varepsilon_1^{1/2} + (1 - f)\varepsilon_2^{1/2}$$	$1.543 + 0.024i$
8	Layered-sphere (Voshchinnikov and Mathis, 1999): $$\varepsilon_{\text{eff}} = \frac{\mathcal{A}_2}{\mathcal{A}_1}^{(**)}$$	$1.523 + 0.022i$
9	Extended effective medium approximation (EEMA) (Chýlek and Videen, 1998; Videen and Chýlek, 1998): $$(\varepsilon_{\text{eff}})_{k+1} = \varepsilon_2 \frac{\mathcal{A}_k(1 - f) + f\mathcal{B}_k}{\mathcal{A}_k(1 - f) - 2f\mathcal{B}_k}^{(***)}$$	—
10	Wiener's bounds (Wiener, 1910): max (Eq. (2.20)) min (Eq. (2.21))	$1.567 + 0.026i$ $1.438 + 0.015i$

f is the volume fraction of the component with dielectric permittivity ε_1;
* Effective refractive index for the mixture with 80% of astrosil ($m = $

1.679 + 0.030i; Table 4) and 20% of vacuum ($m = 1.0 + 0.0i$); [**] $\mathcal{A}_{1,2}$ can be found from Eq. (2.48) with $L_j = 1/3$; [***] The effective optical constants are determined from an iterative procedure, where

$$\mathcal{A}_k = -\frac{12i\pi^2 \varepsilon_{\text{eff}}^{3/2}}{\lambda^3}, \mathcal{B}_k = -\frac{3}{4\pi r_s^3} \sum_{n=1}^{\infty} (2n+1) \left[a_n \left(r_s, \frac{\varepsilon_1}{\varepsilon_{\text{eff}}} \right) + b_n \left(r_s, \frac{\varepsilon_1}{\varepsilon_{\text{eff}}} \right) \right]$$

and a_n, b_n are the Mie scattering coefficients.

So-called extended effective medium approximations (EEMAs) generalizes the classical electrostatic approach for non-Rayleigh inclusion size. All EEMAs are based on the assumption that at least one component is highly absorbing (see the discussion in Chýlek *et al.*, 2000).

The last column in Table 5 contains the values of the effective refractive index of the mixture with 80% of astrosil and 20% of vacuum which were calculated using different mixing rules. The obtained indices are similar. This demonstrates that the choice of mixing rule is unimportant in given case. Figure 5 shows variations of the refractive indices for amorphous carbon and astrosil with the porosity. The type of mixtures when the inclusion permittivity is smaller than the matrix permittivity resembles "Swiss cheese" while the inverse case (like carbon in silicate) is similar to "raisin pudding". Figure 5 illustrates that even a rather small fraction of vacuum can result in noticeable changes in n and k. Several other mixing rules were reviewed and compared by Sihvola (1999).

There exist certain limits of possible values of effective permittivity values for a given mixture (see Aspnes, 1982; Petrov, 1986 and Kärkkäinen *et al.*, 1999 for discussion). The absolute bounds[5] to ε_{eff} were given by Wiener (1910)

$$\varepsilon_{\text{eff, max}} = f\varepsilon_1 + (1 - f)\varepsilon_2, \tag{2.20}$$

and

$$\frac{1}{\varepsilon_{\text{eff, min}}} = \frac{f}{\varepsilon_1} + \frac{1 - f}{\varepsilon_2}. \tag{2.21}$$

---

[5] These expressions were exactly derived for non-absorbing materials but it seems they can be applied to slightly absorbing materials too.

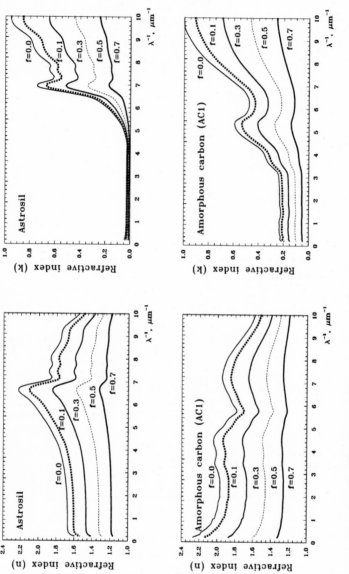

Figure 5 Wavelength dependence of the refractive indices of two materials with a different fraction of vacuum ($f = 0\text{--}0.7$) calculated with the Bruggeman mixing rule.

These two cases correspond to capacitors that are connected in parallel or series in circuit. For any composition and microstructure, ε_{eff} must lie on or within the region in the complex plane confined by Eqs. (2.20) and (2.21) as long as the microstructural dimensions remain small compared with the radiation wavelength.

For a statistically homogeneous and isotropic mixture, Hashin and Shtrikman (1962) found other bounds[6]. They are based on a variational treatment of the energy functional for a mixture with the inhomogeneity distributed in three dimensions

$$\varepsilon_{\text{eff, max}} = \varepsilon_2 + \cfrac{f}{\cfrac{1}{\varepsilon_1 - \varepsilon_2} + \cfrac{1 - f}{3\varepsilon_2}} \qquad (2.22)$$

and

$$\varepsilon_{\text{eff, min}} = \varepsilon_1 + \cfrac{1 - f}{\cfrac{1}{\varepsilon_2 - \varepsilon_1} + \cfrac{f}{3\varepsilon_1}}, \qquad (2.23)$$

where it is assumed that $\varepsilon_2 < \varepsilon_1$. The bounds can serve for a check of old and new EMTs.

The mixing rules can also be extended to multi-component mixtures (in some cases this is evident) and for a non-spherical shape of inclusions (see, e.g., Ossenkopf, 1991; Stognienko et al., 1995).

A special question is the range of applicability of the EMTs. EMTs' predictions can be compared with laboratory measurements of the refractive index of a composite material or the scattering properties of a grain (see Sect. 2.2.5) and numerical results obtained using light scattering theory (Sect. 2.2.3). Unfortunately, the creation of multi-component samples with abundances resembling the cosmic ones is an unfeasible problem. The numerical technique to calculate the optical properties of composite particles is very complicated and extremely computational time consuming. Therefore, systematic studies of the accuracy of different EMTs are absent although attempts to find the "best" EMT have been made several times (e.g., Jones, 1988; Hage and Greenberg, 1990; Lumme and Rahola, 1994).

---

[6] A generalization of the bounds of Wiener and Hashin and Shtrikman was suggested by Milton (1980).

Chýlek and Videen (1998) and Videen and Chýlek (1998) considered the model of a non-absorbing sphere with an arbitrarily located highly absorbing spherical inclusion. Wolff *et al.* (1994, 1998) analyzed the optical properties of silicate particles with different degrees of porosity. In both cases, the size of inclusions was changed that gave the possibility of considering both Rayleigh and non-Rayleigh inclusions. A general conclusion is that an EMT agrees well with the exact theory if the inclusions are Rayleigh and their volume fraction f is below $\sim$ 40–60%. However, in the case of non-Rayleigh inclusions, apparently, f should not exceed $\sim$10%. Note also that the accuracy of calculations of different optical characteristics with the same EMT is distinguished: the results for extinction and scattering cross-sections[7] are usually the most precise.

Kolokolova and Gustafson (2001) recommend of using EMTs if the volume fraction of inclusions is not more than 10%. They performed a comprehensive study of the possibility of applying nine mixing rules comparing calculations for organic spheres with silicate inclusions with microwave analog experiments (see Sect. 2.2.5). The comparison included the angular distribution and wavelength dependence of intensity and polarization of scattered light. In particular, it is found that all EMTs fit the experiments in the forward scattering domain (for scattering angles $\Theta = 0°$–$20°$). EMTs can be used for rough estimates of intensity and polarization at $\Theta = 60°$–$120°$ and do not well in the backscattering domain or within the range $\Theta = 30°$–$70°$. The values of polarization calculated using EMTs will most likely be overestimated.

An interesting paper was published by Spanier and Herman (2000) who measured the reflectance of the porous silicon carbide thin films on SiC substrates in the wavelength range 9–16 μm. The experimental results were compared with model calculations using several EMTs. Because the porosity was rather large (the fraction of vacuum $f = 0.50 - 0.74$), any EMT alone could not reproduce the experiments. However, a hybrid model using the linear combination of the modified Garnett and Looyenga's mixing rules (see Table 5) was found to be in very good agreement with the measurements.

---

[7] See definitions in Sect. 2.2.1.

2.2   Equipment

When provision (the optical constants) are laid in, it must be converted using special equipment (light scattering theory) into *optical properties* of particles: various cross-sections, scattering matrix, etc. The scheme of transformation and input/output parameters are shown in Fig. 6. There are various methods of conversion and the choice of equipment depends on the required accuracy and available computational capacities. The simplest way is to use the products in

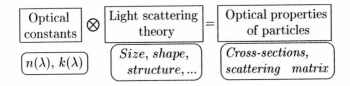

Figure 6 Scheme of transformation of the optical constants into the optical properties.

the initial form. From the point of light scattering, this corresponds to the Rayleigh (electrostatic) approximation (see Sect. 2.2.4). In this case, the optical constants arise directly in expressions for light scattering characteristics (e.g., Eq. (2.59)). However, it is not worth of forgetting the final goal because campfire suits the preparation of meat but not a cake. From the other side, the thorough application of a refining technique like a modern grill or microwave oven is not always justified since it may lead to starvation. The last remark is related to very complicated modern light scattering methods which cannot be applied to astronomical calculations in a reasonable computational time.

The theory of light scattering by small particles makes it possible to calculate:

- intensity and polarization of radiation scattered in any direction;

- energy absorbed or emitted by a grain and to find its temperature;

- emission spectra of dusty objects;

- motion of dust grains under the action of radiation pressure force.

2.2.1 General definitions

Light scattering theory operates with incident $(\vec{E}^{(0)}, \vec{H}^{(0)})$ and scattered $(\vec{E}^{(1)}, \vec{H}^{(1)})$ electromagnetic fields and the field inside a particle (internal field; $\vec{E}^{(2)}, \vec{H}^{(2)}$). A particle distorts (deforms) the incident radiation field. Scattering is usually considered in the Cartesian coordinate system (see Fig. 7), the incident and scattered wavevectors define the *scattering plane*. Here Θ and Φ are the scattering ($0° \leq \Theta \leq 180°$) and azimuthal ($0° \leq \Phi \leq 360°$) angles

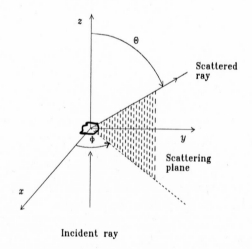

Figure 7 Scattering by an arbitrary particle, Θ – the scattering angle, Φ – the azimuthal angle.

in the reference system related to the scattering plane (laboratory frame). The incident and scattered rays are characterized by the corresponding unit vectors. Vectors $\vec{E}^{(0),(1)}$ can be divided into the components parallel and perpendicular to the scattering plane: $E_{\parallel}^{(0),(1)} = E_{TM}^{(0),(1)}$, $E_{\perp}^{(0),(1)} = E_{TE}^{(0),(1)}$, where the subscripts TM and TE relate to two (transverse magnetic and transverse electric) modes of polarization of incident or scattered radiation (Bohren and Huffman, 1983).

The connection between the components of incident and scattered radiation is given by the matrix expression

$$\left(\begin{array}{c} E_{\parallel}^{(1)} \\ E_{\perp}^{(1)} \end{array} \right) = -\frac{e^{ik(R-\vec{R})}}{ikR} \left(\begin{array}{cc} T_{22}(\Theta,\Phi) & T_{12}(\Theta,\Phi) \\ T_{21}(\Theta,\Phi) & T_{11}(\Theta,\Phi) \end{array} \right) \left(\begin{array}{c} E_{\parallel}^{(0)} \\ E_{\perp}^{(0)} \end{array} \right),$$
(2.24)

where R is the distance from a particle to observer and the elements of the *amplitude (Jones) matrix* $T_{ij}(\Theta,\Phi)$ are determined by the properties of the scatterer. They are calculated on the basis of light scattering theory for a given particle size, shape, structure and orientation (see Fig. 6).

Since one measures intensity (flux) of scattered light but not its amplitude, the connection between the *Stokes vectors* of the incident and scattered radiation is usually considered. It is described by the *scattering (Müller) matrix*

$$\left(\begin{array}{c} I \\ Q \\ U \\ V \end{array} \right) = \frac{1}{k^2 R^2} \left(\begin{array}{cccc} F_{11} & F_{12} & F_{13} & F_{14} \\ F_{21} & F_{22} & F_{23} & F_{24} \\ F_{31} & F_{32} & F_{33} & F_{34} \\ F_{41} & F_{42} & F_{43} & F_{44} \end{array} \right) \left(\begin{array}{c} I_0 \\ Q_0 \\ U_0 \\ V_0 \end{array} \right).$$
(2.25)

The elements of the amplitude and scattering matrices are related (van de Hulst, 1957; Bohren and Huffman, 1983).

The scattering matrix is widely applied to the description of an *arbitrary* scattering, absorbing or refracting medium or device. The elements of the matrix may be measured with the aid of the combination of a linear polarizer and linear retarder (Tinbergen, 1996). Only 7 of 16 elements in the scattering matrix are independent. There exist nine relations between the elements and numerous relations for check-up (see Hovenier, 1994 for details).

The degree and positional angle of linear polarization of scattered radiation are

$$P = \frac{\sqrt{Q^2 + U^2}}{I} = \frac{\sqrt{F_{21}^2 + F_{31}^2}}{F_{11}}, \tag{2.26}$$

and

$$\vartheta = \frac{1}{2} \arctan \frac{U}{Q} = \frac{1}{2} \arctan \frac{F_{31}}{F_{21}}. \tag{2.27}$$

The degree of circular polarization is determined by the Stokes parameter V

$$q = \frac{V}{I} = \frac{F_{41}}{F_{11}}. \tag{2.28}$$

The right-hand parts in Eqs. (2.26)–(2.28) are obtained from Eq. (2.25) in the case of the non-polarized incident radiation when the Stokes vector of the incident radiation is $(I_0, Q_0, U_0, V_0) = (1, 0, 0, 0)$.

Neglecting the polarization in Eq. (2.25), we can write

$$I = \frac{F_{11}(\Theta, \Phi)}{k^2 R^2} I_0 = \frac{F(\Theta, \Phi)}{k^2 R^2} I_0, \tag{2.29}$$

where $F_{11}(\Theta, \Phi)$ or $F(\Theta, \Phi)$ is the *phase function* (scattering diagram). Integrating the scattered radiation over all directions we can find the total scattered energy. It is equal to the energy incident on the particle surface C_{sca}, i.e.

$$C_{sca} = \int_{4\pi} \frac{F(\Theta, \Phi)}{k^2} \, d\omega = \int_0^{2\pi} \int_0^{\pi} \frac{F(\Theta, \Phi)}{k^2} \sin\Theta \, d\Theta \, d\Phi. \tag{2.30}$$

Equation (2.30) defines the *total scattering cross-section C_{sca}*, while $F(\Theta, \Phi)/k^2$ is the *differential scattering cross-section*. This equation is used for normalization of the phase function

$$\frac{1}{4\pi} \int_{4\pi} \mathcal{F} \, d\omega = 1 = \frac{1}{4\pi} \int_{4\pi} \frac{F(\Theta, \Phi)}{k^2 C_{sca}} \, d\omega, \tag{2.31}$$

where $\mathcal{F}$ is the normalized phase function (or $x(\gamma)$ in the radiative transfer literature, see e.g. Sobolev, 1975).

The summary reduction of the intensity of transmitted radiation due to scattering and absorption is called *extinction*. The *extinction cross-section C_{ext}* is determined from the *optical theorem* which is valid for scattering of any kind: electromagnetic, acoustic, particle. This theorem establishes the relation between C_{ext} and the scattering amplitude in the forward direction $T(0°, 0°) = 1/2[T_{22}(0°, 0°) + T_{11}(0°, 0°)]$ (see Eq. (2.24))

$$C_{ext} = \frac{4\pi}{k^2} \operatorname{Re}\{T(0°, 0°)\}. \tag{2.32}$$

The extinction cross-section is the sum of the scattering and absorption ones

$$C_{ext} = C_{sca} + C_{abs}. \tag{2.33}$$

The ratio of the scattering to extinction cross-section is called the particle *albedo* (or single scattering albedo)

$$\Lambda = \frac{C_{sca}}{C_{ext}} = \frac{C_{sca}}{C_{sca} + C_{abs}}, \tag{2.34}$$

which varies in the limits $0 < \Lambda \leq 1$. The maximum value $\Lambda = 1$ corresponds to non-absorbing particles when the imaginary part of refractive index $k = 0$ (in this case $C_{abs} = 0$ and $C_{ext} = C_{sca}$).

Radiation transfers the momentum and it is important to consider the *radiation pressure* cross-sections

$$C_{pr} = C_{ext} - \langle\cos\Theta\rangle C_{sca} = C_{abs} + (1 - \langle\cos\Theta\rangle)C_{sca}, \tag{2.35}$$

where C_{ext} is proportional to the momentum deleted from the beam and $\langle\cos\Theta\rangle C_{sca}$ is the recoil momentum of the scattered radiation.

The *asymmetry parameter* $\langle\cos\Theta\rangle$ (or g[8]) describes the asymmetry of the phase function

$$g = \langle\cos\Theta\rangle = \frac{\int_{4\pi} F(\Theta, \Phi)\cos\Theta\, d\omega}{\int_{4\pi} F(\Theta, \Phi)\, d\omega}. \tag{2.36}$$

It varies from –1 (mirror particles) to 1 (all radiation is forward scattered) and is equal to 0 if the scattered radiation is azimuthal independent and symmetric with respect to the plane perpendicular to the incident radiation.

---

[8] This notation is related to the Henyey–Greenstein phase function that is very often use in radiative transfer modelling (see Sect. 2.3.2).

All cross-sections C are connected with the corresponding *efficiency factors Q* via the relation

$$C = GQ, \qquad (2.37)$$

where G is the geometrical ("viewing") cross-section of a particle (the area of the particle shadow). The efficiency factors show the fraction of energy removed from the beam by the particle in comparison with that by a screen with area G.

2.2.2 Spheres versus non-spheres

Numerous polarimetric observations (interstellar polarization, polarized thermal emission, wavelength dependence of the positional angle of polarization observed in red giants, etc.) cannot be explained using spherical grains only, and light scattering by non-spherical particles must be involved. In many astronomical applications, it seems to be sufficient to calculate the optical properties of *spheroids* — one of the simplest non-spherical particles of finite size.

Spheroids are the ellipsoids of revolution obtaining when an ellipse rotates around its major (prolate spheroid) or minor (oblate spheroid) axis. The shape of spheroidal particles is characterized by the aspect ratio a/b where a and b are the major and minor semiaxes (see Fig. 8). By changing a/b the particles with a shape varying from close to a sphere ($a/b \simeq 1$) up to needles (prolate spheroids) or disks (oblate spheroids) can be studied.

The particle size can be specified by the parameters $x_V = 2\pi r_V/\lambda$ (r_V is the radius of a sphere whose volume is equal to that of the spheroid, λ the wavelength of incident radiation) or $c = 2\pi/\lambda \cdot d/2$ (d is the focal distance of a spheroid) and also by the parameter $2\pi a/\lambda$. The expressions relating these parameters have the form

$$\frac{2\pi a}{\lambda} = \left(\frac{a}{b}\right)^{(1-\hat{f})/2} c\xi_0, \qquad (2.38)$$

$$x_V = \frac{2\pi r_V}{\lambda} = \frac{2\pi a}{\lambda}\left(\frac{a}{b}\right)^{-(\hat{f}+3)/6}, \qquad (2.39)$$

where $\hat{f} = 1$ and $r_V^3 = ab^2$ for prolate spheroids and $\hat{f} = -1$ and $r_V^3 = a^2b$ for oblate ones.

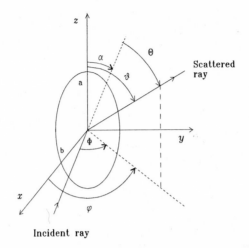

Incident ray

Figure 8 Scattering geometry for a prolate homogeneous spheroid. The origin of the coordinate system is at the center of the spheroid while the z-axis coincides with the particle rotation axis. The angle of incidence α is that between the direction of incidence and the z-axis in the x–z-plane. The direction of the scattered wave in the far-field zone is represented by the angles θ, φ in the spherical coordinate system related to the spheroid's rotation axis (particle frame) or by the angles Θ, Φ in the reference system related to the scattering plane (laboratory frame).

The parameter ξ_0 depends only on the aspect ratio a/b

$$\xi_0 = \left(\frac{a}{b}\right)^{(1+\hat{f})/2} \left[\left(\frac{a}{b}\right)^2 - 1\right]^{-1/2}. \qquad (2.40)$$

The geometrical cross-section of spheroids (see Eq. (2.37)) is

$$G(\alpha) = \pi b \left(a^2 \sin^2 \alpha + b^2 \cos^2 \alpha\right)^{1/2} \quad \text{for prolate spheroids} \quad (2.41)$$

and

$$G(\alpha) = \pi a \left(a^2 \cos^2 \alpha + b^2 \sin^2 \alpha\right)^{1/2} \quad \text{for oblate spheroids.} \quad (2.42)$$

In order to compare the optical properties of the particles of different shapes it is convenient to consider the ratios of the cross-sections for spheroids to the geometrical cross-sections of the equal volume spheres, $C/\pi r_V^2$. They can be found as

$$\frac{C}{\pi r_V^2} = \frac{[(a/b)^2 \sin^2 \alpha + \cos^2 \alpha]^{1/2}}{(a/b)^{2/3}} Q \qquad (2.43)$$

for a prolate spheroid and

$$\frac{C}{\pi r_V^2} = \frac{[(a/b)^2 \cos^2 \alpha + \sin^2 \alpha]^{1/2}}{(a/b)^{1/3}} Q \qquad (2.44)$$

for an oblate spheroid.

The difference in the single light scattering by a spherical particle and aligned non-spherical (spheroidal) particle are clearly seen from Table 6. It shows the behaviour of the elements of the first column in the scattering matrix (Eq. (2.25)) which determine the scattered radiation if the incident radiation is non-polarized. Corresponding

Table 6 Features of non-polarized light scattering by aligned non-spherical (spheroidal) particles.

Spherical particles	Spheroids (oblique incident radiation, $\alpha \neq 0°$)
no azimuthal dependence of scattered radiation: $F_{11}(\Theta)$	azimuthal dependence of scattered radiation: $F_{11}(\Theta, \Phi)$
no polarization in forward and backward directions: $F_{21}(0°) = 0$, $F_{21}(180°) = 0$	linear polarization in forward and backward directions: $F_{21}(0°, 0°) \neq 0$, $F_{21}(180°, 180°) \neq 0$
no rotation of positional angle of linear polarization: $F_{31}(\Theta) = 0$	rotation of positional angle of linear polarization: $F_{31}(\Theta, \Phi) \neq 0$ if $\Phi \neq 0°, 180°$
no circular polarization after first scattering: $F_{41}(\Theta) = 0$	circular polarization after first scattering: $F_{41}(\Theta, \Phi) \neq 0$ if $\Phi \neq 0°$, $180°$ and $\Theta \neq 0°, 180°$

illustrations are given in Part II, Sect. 6. Other possibilities for diagnostics of particle shape like the inequality of elements F_{11} and F_{22}[9]
(for spheres $F_{11} = F_{22}$) appear in the cases of polarized incident radiation or multiple light scattering. But frequently such measurements
of radiation from astronomical objects cannot be performed easily.

2.2.3   Exact methods

Theoretical approaches to solve the light scattering problem are divided into "exact methods" and "approximations" by their dependence
on:

1. the size parameter $x = 2\pi r/\lambda$, where r is the typical size of a
   particle (e.g., the radius of the equivolume sphere) and λ the
   wavelength of incident radiation in the surrounding medium;

2. the module of the difference between the refractive index and
   unity $|m - 1|$;

3. the phase shift $\rho = 2x|m - 1|$.

The approximations act if at least two of these quantities are much
smaller or much larger than unity (van de Hulst, 1957). In particular, approximate approaches allow one to estimate the wavelength
dependence of extinction cross-sections easily. The latter determine,
for example, interstellar extinction $A(\lambda)$ (see Sect. 3.2). Already early multi-colour observations showed that $A(\lambda) \propto \lambda^{-1}$ in the visible
part of spectrum and *any approximation does not predict such wavelength dependence.* Therefore, *astronomers in general are doomed to
work with exact methods.*

Spherical grains do not explain the interstellar polarization and
another feature required of the theory is the ability to treat non-
spherical particles with sizes close to or larger than the radiation
wavelength. The methods and technique of calculating light scattering by non-spherical particles were rapidly developed in recent
years. They are described in special issues of *Journal of Quantita-
tive Spectroscopy and Radiative Transfer* (Hovenier, 1996; Lumme,

---

[9] See discussion in the paper of Mishchenko and Travis (1994a).

1998; Mishchenko *et al.*, 1999; Videen *et al.*, 2001; Kolokolova *et al.*, 2003), review papers (Wriedt, 1998; A.R. Jones, 1999), the collective monograph (Mishchenko *et al.*, 2000a) and the book of Mishchenko *et al.* (2002). The comprehensive consideration of spherical particles including inhomogeneous and anisotropic ones was published by Babenko *et al.* (2003).

At present, only a few methods satisfy astronomical demands and three of them are widely used in modelling. They are: the separation of variables method for spheroids, the T-matrix method for axially symmetric particles and some modifications of the method of momentum (and first of all the discrete dipole approximation). Note that the first method is based on differential formulation of the light scattering problem whereas the two others are surface and volume integral equation methods, respectively.

Separation of Variables Method (SVM). SVM is the classical method. Historically, it was the first method used to solve the light scattering problem for a particle whose size was comparable to the wavelength of incident radiation (Mie, 1908; Debye, 1909). Mie's theory presents a solution to the Helmholtz equation in the spherical coordinate system. The solution in the cylindrical coordinate system gives the simplest solution for non-spherical particles — infinitely long circular cylinders. The Helmholtz equation can also be solved in a spheroidal coordinate system. In this case, the scattering coefficients are bound in infinite systems of linear algebraic equations and can be calculated from truncated systems. For spheres, infinitely long cylinders and spheroids, solutions for core-mantle and multi-layered confocal particles were also obtained. The main steps of SVM's development are shown in Table 7. It includes the solutions found for particles with an arbitrary complex refractive index m.

The SVM is based on the consideration of the vector wave equation in a special coordinate system. The surface of the particle has to coincide with one of the coordinate surfaces. This tight connection specifies the principal *disadvantage* of all the SVM solutions: the impossibility of considering particles of arbitrary shape and structure. The main *advantage* of SVM solutions is the higher accuracy of numerical results in comparison with more universal methods.

Table 7 Solutions to the light scattering problem obtained by the separation of variables method.

Particle	Author(s)
Sphere:	
homogeneous	Mie (1908)
	Debye (1909)
core-mantle	Aden and Kerker (1951)
	Shifrin (1952)
	Güttler (1952)
multi-layered	Wait (1963)
	Wu and Wang (1991) (recursive procedure)
Infinitely long circular cylinder:	
homogeneous	Lord Rayleigh (1881) (perpendicular incidence)
	Wait (1955) (oblique incidence)
	Lind and Greenberg (1966) (oblique incidence)
core-mantle	Shah (1970)
multi-layered	Yeh and Lindgren (1977) (perpendicular incidence)
	Barabas (1987) (oblique incidence)
	Gurwich *et al.* (1999) (recursive procedure)
Spheroid:	
homogeneous	Asano and Yamamoto (1975)
	Farafonov (1983)*; Voshchinnikov and and Farafonov (1985, 1993)
core-mantle	Onaka (1980)
	Farafonov (1994a)*; Farafonov *et al.* (1996)
multi-layered	Gurwich *et al.* (2000*, 2003) (recursive procedure)
	Farafonov (2001)* (recursive procedure)

* Theory without numerical results

All the solutions given by the SVM are based on calculations of the corresponding special functions (spherical, cylindrical, spheroidal). This mainly determines the computational limits of the solutions. Other computations are rather simple and include summation of series or solution of systems of linear equations.

The solutions to the electromagnetic problem for spheroids published by Asano and Yamamoto (1975) and Farafonov (1983) (see also Voshchinnikov and Farafonov, 1993) are fundamentally distinguished. In the former, the authors used the Debye potentials to present the electromagnetic fields. This approach is similar to the Mie solution for spheres. Farafonov chose special combinations of the Debye and Hertz potentials, i.e. the potentials used in the solutions for spheres and infinitely long cylinders, respectively. All the electromagnetic fields were divided into two parts: the axisymmetric part not depending on the azimuthal angle φ, and the non-axisymmetric part when the integration over φ gives zero. This approach has an incontestable advantage for strongly elongated or flattened particles (see Sect. 3.2.1). It should also be noted that the convergence of Farafonov's solution for spheroids follows that of the Mie solution for spheres (see Table 2 in Voshchinnikov, 1996).

T-Matrix Method (TMM). Another name for this approach is the Extended Boundary Conditions Method (EBCM). It was developed by Waterman (1971). An alternative derivation of the method was given by Barber and Yeh (1975). It may work for arbitrary shaped particles, but was mainly applied to axisymmetric ones: finite cylinders, spheroids, Chebyshev particles, bispheres.

The main idea of the method is an expansion of the incident, internal and scattered radiation fields in terms of the vector spherical harmonic functions. Because of linearity of the Maxwell equations, the relations between the expansion coefficients of the fields are linear and given by two matrices. Thus, the solution consists of calculations of the matrix elements which are the surface integrals and inversion of one of the matrices. The *advantages* of the approach are simple compact codes and their high speed. Another advantage is the ability to treat a more complex case of elastic waves, the possible applicability to particles of complex shapes, and available analytical averaging over the particle orientations within the expansion coefficients which can greatly enlarge the method efficiency for ensembles of non-spherical particles. However, for particles whose shapes strongly deviate from the spherical one ($a/b \gtrsim 3$) the TMM does not work well.

To get rid of this defect of the TMM, Lakhtakia *et al.* (1983) and Iskander and Lakhtakia (1984) represented the internal field by several subdomain spherical function expansions centred on the major axis of elongated scatterer. These subdomain expansions are linked to each other by being explicitly matched in the appropriate overlapping zones. This modification led to a considerable increase of the computational time but permitted the consideration of the light scattering by particles with aspect ratios as large as 17.

Another attempt to compel to make the TMM work for highly elongated particles was undertaken by Farafonov et al. (1999). The scattering problem is formulated in the integral form as in the TMM but the fields are divided into two parts like in the SVM solution of Farafonov. The scalar potentials are expanded in terms of the spherical wave functions. The coefficients of the expansions are determined from the solution of algebraic systems similar to those obtained in the TMM. Thus, the new approach should combine the strong aspects of the basic methods: the simple solution scheme typical of the TMM and the ability to treat particles whose shape can be very elongated or flattened as in the SVM. Unfortunately, hopes were not justified: the advantage of the new TMM in the comparison with the traditional one was insignificant (Farafonov and Il'in, 2001).

Generalization of several modifications of the TMM on multi-layered scatterers and the connection between the TMM and the SVM were considered by Farafonov et al. (2003).

The applicability of the TMM was analytically and numerically investigated by Il'in et al. (2004). They showed that the application of the method to the near-field and far-field zones was mathematically correct under different conditions. In the first case, the Rayleigh hypothesis about the convergence of the field expansions everywhere up to the scatterer border must be satisfied. For example, for spheroids this occurs if and only if the aspect ratio $a/b < \sqrt{2}$. In the second case, the condition is essentially weaker and for spheroids it is satisfied always. In other words, one can use the TMM to calculate the characteristics of the scattered radiation in the far-field zone (i.e. cross-sections, scattering matrix elements, etc.) for spheroids with any aspect ratios. However, such calculations may require very large computational efforts (Mishchenko and Travis, 1994b; Zakharova and Mishchenko, 2000).

Discrete Dipole Approximation (DDA). This technique can calculate the optical properties of particles of arbitrary shapes and/or of inhomogeneous structure. Since the formulation of the DDA by Purcell and Pennypacker (1973), the method has been rediscovered, reformulated and extended several times.

In most formulations of the DDA a particle with the bulk dielectric constant ε is replaced by an array of N cubic volume elements or, equivalently, by an assembly of N polarizable "atoms" in vacuum.

The great *advantage* of the DDA its the ability to treat arbitrary shaped particles, anisotropic particles and particles with inhomogeneous structure — the method seems to be the most universal at present. However, two problems may restrict its applications. First, it has relatively low accuracy and second, it is hard to use the method for particles whose size is greater than the wavelength of incident radiation wavelength because of huge memory and computational time demands. The calculations for highly absorbing particles are rather problematical.

A detailed review of the DDA and its applications is given by Draine (2000).

A comparison of methods. Apparently, it is of no sense to compare the methods for particles of the simplest shapes — spheres and infinite cylinders. There exist many different numerical codes and the only question is the maximum size parameter which can be reached with a given code. For homogeneous spheres, the most popular computer program is BHMIE from the book of Bohren and Huffman (1983). However, its upper limit in the x-value is several hundred. At the same time, it is rather easy to write a fast and simple numerical code with practically unlimited maximum size parameter (see computer program NVVMIE in Sect. 5.3).

Different aspects of light scattering methods for non-spherical particles have been discussed several times (Hovenier *et al.*, 1996; Wriedt and Comberg, 1998; Mishchenko *et al.*, 2000b; Voshchinnikov *et al.*, 2000; Il'in *et al.*, 2002; Mishchenko *et al.*, 2002). It is possible to compare the methods from the point of view of the memory and computational time demands, accuracy, applicability to particles of different shape. But as was noted by Mishchenko *et al.* (2000b) "there is no single technique that provides the best results in all cases".

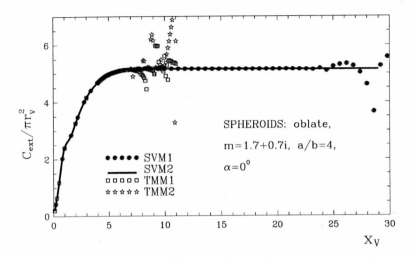

Figure 9 Normalized extinction cross-sections against size parameter x_V for oblate spheroids (see Eq. (2.44)) with the refractive index $m = 1.7 + 0.7i$, $a/b = 4$ and $\alpha = 0°$. The solutions of Asano and Yamamoto (Rogers and Martin, 1979; Kim and Martin, 1995) [SVM1], Farafonov (Voshchinnikov and Farafonov, 1993) [SVM2], the T-matrix codes of Barber and Hill (1990) [TMM1] and Mishchenko (Mishchenko *et al.*, 1996) [TMM2] were used in the calculations. After Voshchinnikov *et al.* (2000).

With the goal of creating benchmark results for absorbing spheroids, Voshchinnikov *et al.* (2000) considered four different numerical codes. A crude impression of the range of applicability of the methods may be obtained from Fig. 9 where the normalized cross-sections are plotted for oblate spheroids with $m = 1.7 + 0.7i$ and $a/b = 4$. In all cases double precision calculations were used. It should be noted that the advantage of the T-matrix codes appears mainly for particles more spherical than presented in Fig. 9. On the other hand, for larger aspect ratios, the method of Voshchinnikov and Farafonov (1993; SVM2) becomes unrivalled.

Similar computations to those shown in Fig. 9 can also be made using the DDA technique, however, accuracy of calculations by this method is usually essentially lower than those by the SVM and TMM (Hovenier *et al.*, 1996; see also discussion in Andersen *et al.*, 2002,

2003). The restrictions of the modern version of the DDA are given by Draine (2000) who recommends its use for targets with dimensions $r/\lambda \lesssim 5$ and refractive indices $|m - 1| \lesssim 3$. Recently, Collinge and Draine (2003) introduced a new DDA polarizability prescription which provided an increase in accuracy over previous approaches, especially for highly absorbing materials.

2.2.4 Approximations

The most popular approximation is that of Lord *Rayleigh* (other names are the electrostatic or long wavelength approximation) whose applicability is defined by two conditions (van de Hulst, 1957; Bohren and Huffman, 1983): $x \ll 1$ and $|m|x \ll 1$. It works at the infrared where various dusty bands are observed. The refractive index increases within the bands (see Fig. 3), but the same accuracy of the Rayleigh approximation can be reached in the band in comparison with the neighboring continuum for particles of smaller sizes.

If $|m - 1| \ll 1$ and $|m - 1|x \ll 1$, the particles are called *optically soft* and their optical properties can be calculated with the *Rayleigh–Gans* approximation. In astronomical applications it is widely used in the X-ray region (Part II, Sect. 6) where the refractive indices of all materials are close to unity (Sect. 2.1.2).

A generalization of the Rayleigh and Rayleigh–Gans approximations is the *quasistatic approximation*. In this approximation, the electromagnetic field inside a particle is represented by the incident field (as in the Rayleigh–Gans approximation) taking into account the polarizibility of the particle (as in the Rayleigh approximation).

Quasistatic approximation for spheroidal particles. Here we consider the quasistatic approximation for spheroidal particles. The expressions for the efficiency factors and amplitude matrices were obtained by Farafonov (1994b).

In the quasistatic approximation, a solution can be found both in the *laboratory frame*, where the angles of the scattered radiation Θ, Φ are related to the scattering plane, and in the *particle frame*, where the angles θ, φ are related to the spheroid's rotation axis (Figs. 7, 8).

The elements of the amplitude matrix (Eq. (2.24)) in the particle system are:

$$\left\{ \begin{aligned} &T_{11} = \mathcal{K}\tilde{\alpha}_1 \cos\varphi \, G(u) \\[6pt] &T_{12} = \mathcal{K}\tilde{\alpha}_1 \cos\theta \sin\varphi \, G(u) \\[6pt] &T_{21} = -\mathcal{K}\tilde{\alpha}_1 \cos\alpha \sin\varphi \, G(u) \\[6pt] &T_{22} = \mathcal{K}(\tilde{\alpha}_3 \sin\alpha \sin\theta + \tilde{\alpha}_1 \cos\alpha \cos\theta \cos\varphi) \, G(u), \end{aligned} \right. \tag{2.45}$$

where

$$\mathcal{K} = -\frac{i}{3}(c\xi_0)^3 \left(\frac{a}{b}\right)^{-2\hat{f}},$$

$$G(u) = \frac{3}{u^3}(\sin u - u \cos u)$$

and

$$u = c\xi_0 \left[(\cos\theta - \cos\alpha)^2 + \left(\frac{a}{b}\right)^{-2\hat{f}} (\sin^2\theta \right.$$

$$\left. + \sin^2\alpha - 2\sin\theta \sin\alpha \cos\varphi)\right]^{1/2}.$$

In Eq. (2.45) $\tilde{\alpha}_j$ is the polarizability along each principal axis, $j \, (\equiv x, y, z)$, $\tilde{\alpha}_1 = \tilde{\alpha}_2$; the asterisk denotes the complex conjugation. The polarizability of homogeneous spheroids is

$$\tilde{\alpha}_j = \frac{\varepsilon - 1}{L_j(\varepsilon - 1) + 1}. \tag{2.46}$$

For N-layered confocal spheroids, $\tilde{\alpha}_j$ is (Farafonov, 2000)

$$\tilde{\alpha}_j = V \frac{\mathcal{A}_2 - \mathcal{A}_1}{3[(\mathcal{A}_2 - \mathcal{A}_1)L_j + \mathcal{A}_1]}, \tag{2.47}$$

$$\begin{pmatrix} \mathcal{A}_1 \\ \mathcal{A}_2 \end{pmatrix} = \begin{pmatrix} 1 & L_j \\ \tilde{\varepsilon}_N & \tilde{\varepsilon}_N(L_j - 1) \end{pmatrix}$$

$$\times \prod_{s=2}^{N-1} \begin{pmatrix} (\tilde{\varepsilon}_s - 1)L_j + 1 & (\tilde{\varepsilon}_s - 1)L_j(L_j - 1)/\tilde{V}_j \\ -(\tilde{\varepsilon}_s - 1)\tilde{V}_j & -(\tilde{\varepsilon}_s - 1)(L_j - 1) + 1 \end{pmatrix}$$

$$\times \left(\begin{array}{c} (\tilde{\varepsilon}_1 - 1)L_j + 1 \\ -(\tilde{\varepsilon}_1 - 1)\tilde{V}_1 \end{array} \right), \qquad (2.48)$$

where $\tilde{\varepsilon}_s = \varepsilon_s/\varepsilon_{s+1}$ is the relative dielectric constant ($\varepsilon = m^2$) of the layers (s, $s + 1$) and $\tilde{V}_s = (a_s b_s c_s)/(abc)$ the ratio of the volume of the s-th ellipsoid to the total volume of the particle. Assuming the vacuum as a surrounding medium, the $\tilde{\varepsilon}_N$ for the outermost layer is the dielectric constant ε_N.

The geometrical factors are calculated from the following expressions:

$$L_3 = \frac{1 - e^2}{e^2} \left(\frac{1}{2e} \ln \frac{1 + e}{1 - e} - 1 \right), \qquad e = \sqrt{1 - b^2/a^2} \qquad (2.49)$$

for prolate spheroids and

$$L_3 = \frac{1 + \tilde{e}^2}{\tilde{e}^2} \left(1 - \frac{1}{\tilde{e}^2} \arctan \tilde{e} \right), \qquad \tilde{e} = \sqrt{a^2/b^2 - 1}, \qquad (2.50)$$

for oblate spheroids, where

$$L_1 = L_2 = \frac{1 - L_3}{2}. \qquad (2.51)$$

The elements of the amplitude matrix in the laboratory system are:

$$\left\{ \begin{array}{l} \tilde{T}_{11} = \mathcal{K}[\tilde{\alpha}_1 + (\tilde{\alpha}_3 - \tilde{\alpha}_1) \sin^2 \alpha \sin^2(\Phi - \Phi_0)]\, G(\tilde{u}) \\[2mm] \tilde{T}_{12} = \mathcal{K}(\tilde{\alpha}_3 - \tilde{\alpha}_1) \sin \alpha [\cos \Theta \sin \alpha \cos(\Phi - \Phi_0) \\ \qquad - \sin \Theta \cos \alpha] \sin(\Phi - \Phi_0)\, G(\tilde{u}) \\[2mm] \tilde{T}_{21} = \mathcal{K}(\tilde{\alpha}_3 - \tilde{\alpha}_1) \sin^2 \alpha \cos(\Phi - \Phi_0) \sin(\Phi - \Phi_0)\, G(\tilde{u}) \\[2mm] \tilde{T}_{22} = \mathcal{K}\{\tilde{\alpha}_1 \cos \Theta + (\tilde{\alpha}_3 - \tilde{\alpha}_1) \sin \alpha [\cos \Theta \sin \alpha \cos(\Phi - \Phi_0) \\ \qquad - \sin \Theta \cos \alpha] \cos(\Phi - \Phi_0)\}\, G(\tilde{u}), \end{array} \right.$$

$$(2.52)$$

where $\Phi_0 = 0°$ for a non-rotating particle and

$$\tilde{u} = 2c\xi_0 \sin \frac{\Theta}{2} \sqrt{\cos^2 \beta' + \left(\frac{a}{b} \right)^{-2f} \sin^2 \beta'},$$

$$\cos \beta' = -\cos \alpha \sin \frac{\Theta}{2} + \sin \alpha \cos \frac{\Theta}{2} \cos(\Phi_0 - \Phi).$$

Expressions for the absorption efficiencies in the quasistatic and Rayleigh approximation coincide:

$$Q_{\text{abs}}^{\text{TE}} = \left(Q_{\text{abs}}^{\text{TE}}\right)_{\text{Rayleigh}} = \mathcal{C}_1 \text{Im}\{\tilde{\alpha}_1\}, \qquad (2.53)$$

$$Q_{\text{abs}}^{\text{TM}} = \left(Q_{\text{abs}}^{\text{TM}}\right)_{\text{Rayleigh}} = \mathcal{C}_1 \text{Im}\{\sin^2 \alpha \cdot \tilde{\alpha}_3 + \cos^2 \alpha \cdot \tilde{\alpha}_1\}. \qquad (2.54)$$

Expressions for the scattering efficiencies have the form

$$Q_{\text{sca}}^{\text{TE}} = \mathcal{C}_2 |\tilde{\alpha}_1|^2 \int_0^{2\pi} \int_0^{\pi} (\cos^2 \varphi + \cos^2 \theta \sin^2 \varphi)\, G^2(u) \sin \theta\, d\theta\, d\varphi, \qquad (2.55)$$

$$Q_{\text{sca}}^{\text{TM}} = \mathcal{C}_2 \left[|\tilde{\alpha}_1|^2 \cos^2 \alpha \int_0^{2\pi} \int_0^{\pi} (\sin^2 \varphi + \cos^2 \theta \cos^2 \varphi) \right.$$

$$\times G^2(u) \sin \theta\, d\theta\, d\varphi + |\tilde{\alpha}_3|^2 \sin^2 \alpha \int_0^{2\pi} \int_0^{\pi} G^2(u) \sin^3 \theta\, d\theta\, d\varphi \qquad (2.56)$$

$$\left. + 2\text{Re}\{\tilde{\alpha}_3 \tilde{\alpha}_1^*\} \sin \alpha \cos \alpha \int_0^{2\pi} \int_0^{\pi} G^2(u) \cos \theta \sin^2 \theta \cos \varphi\, d\theta\, d\varphi \right],$$

where

$$\mathcal{C}_1 = \frac{4}{3} c \xi_0 \left(\frac{\xi_0^2 - \hat{f}}{\xi_0^2 - \hat{f} \cos^2 \alpha} \right)^{1/2}$$

and

$$\mathcal{C}_2 = \frac{c^4 \xi_0^2 (\xi_0^2 - \hat{f})^{3/2}}{9\pi (\xi_0^2 - \hat{f} \cos^2 \alpha)^{1/2}}.$$

Equations (2.53)–(2.57) simplify to the known ones in the special cases:

- Rayleigh approximation: $u = 0, G(u) = 1$

$$\left(Q_{\text{sca}}^{\text{TE}}\right)_{\text{Rayleigh}} = 9\pi \mathcal{C}_2 |\tilde{\alpha}_1|^2, \qquad (2.57)$$

$$\left(Q_{\text{sca}}^{\text{TM}}\right)_{\text{Rayleigh}} = \frac{8\pi}{3} \mathcal{C}_2 \left(|\tilde{\alpha}_1|^2 \cos^2 \alpha + |\tilde{\alpha}_3|^2 \sin^2 \alpha \right); \qquad (2.58)$$

- Rayleigh–Gans approximation: $\tilde{\alpha}_1 = \tilde{\alpha}_3 = m^2 - 1$;
- a sphere with radius r_s $(a/b = 1, \xi_0 \to \infty, c\xi_0 \to x_s = 2\pi r_s/\lambda)$:

$$L_j = 1/3, \quad \tilde{\alpha}_1 = \tilde{\alpha}_3 = 3\frac{m^2 - 1}{m^2 + 2},$$

$$Q_{\text{abs}} = 4x \, \text{Im}\left\{\frac{m^2 - 1}{m^2 + 2}\right\}, \quad Q_{\text{sca}} = \frac{8}{3} x^4 \left|\frac{m^2 - 1}{m^2 + 2}\right|; \quad (2.59)$$

- needles and disks $(a/b \gg 1)$:

$$u = c\xi_0 |\cos\theta - \cos\alpha| \qquad (2.60)$$

for extremely prolate spheroids

$$u = c\xi_0 \sqrt{\sin^2\theta + \sin^2\alpha - 2\sin\theta\sin\alpha\cos\varphi} \qquad (2.61)$$

for extremely oblate spheroids.

Figure 10 shows the dependencies of the scattering efficiencies on the size parameter x_V calculated from an exact solution and in the quasistatic and Rayleigh approximations. One can see that they are substantially different and beginning from some size $Q^{\text{Rayleigh}} > Q^{\text{exact}} > Q^{\text{quasistatic}}$. A similar relationship between the efficiency factors takes place for other values of n, a/b and α. The significant advantage of the quasistatic approximation in the case of very elongated and flattened particles should be noted (see discussion in Voshchinnikov and Farafonov, 2002).

The range of applicability of the quasistatic approximation for homogeneous spheroids was studied by Voshchinnikov and Farafonov (2000). They found that a maximum parameter x_V for which both methods yielded the results coinciding within 1%, can be described by the following approximate formulae:

$$x_V \lesssim \frac{0.02 \ln(a/b) + 0.13}{(n-1)^{0.30}} \qquad (2.62)$$

for prolate spheroids and $\alpha = 0°$,

$$x_V \lesssim \frac{0.10}{(n-1)^{0.13\ln(a/b)+0.29}} \qquad (2.63)$$

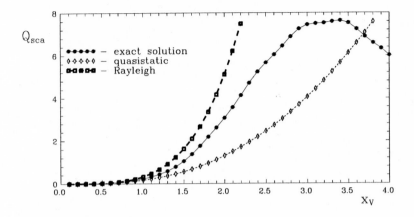

Figure 10 Scattering efficiency factors Q_{sca} for prolate spheroids calculated in the quasistatic and Rayleigh approximations and from the exact solution, $m = 1.5 + 0.0i$, $a/b = 2$, and $\alpha = 0°$. After Voshchinnikov and Farafonov (2000).

for prolate spheroids and $\alpha = 90°$,

$$x_V \lesssim \frac{0.11}{(n-1)^{0.09\ln(a/b)+0.26}} \qquad (2.64)$$

for oblate spheroids and $\alpha = 0°$,

$$x_V \lesssim \frac{0.06\ln(a/b) + 0.12}{(n-1)^{0.23}} \qquad (2.65)$$

for oblate spheroids and $\alpha = 90°$. Implementation of the quasistatic approximation for multi-layered spheroids and ellipsoids is considered by Farafonov *et al.* (2002, 2003).

Note that the applicability of the Rayleigh approximation for spheres was investigated many times. A comprehensive study was done by Ku and Felske (1984) who found, in particular, that the Rayleigh approximation was valid with the 1% accuracy if

$$x \leq 0.238|m|^{-5/3}, \qquad (2.66)$$

where $m = n + ki$ and $k \geq 0.1$.

S-approximation for spheres. In the case of particles larger than the wavelength of incident radiation, it is possible to obtain rather simple expressions for efficiency factors which can be used instead of exact theory, for example, in order to solve the inverse problems (as in the case of modelling of interstellar extinction, see Zubko *et al.*, 1996).

If $|m - 1| \ll 1$ and $x \gg 1$, the theory of *anomalous diffraction* can be applied. Its most useful result is the well-known expression for the extinction efficiency factor of spheres, namely (see van de Hulst, 1957),

$$Q_{\text{ext}}^{\text{vdHA}}(m, x) = 2 - 4\frac{\sin \rho}{\rho} + 4\frac{1 - \cos \rho}{\rho^2}. \qquad (2.67)$$

This so-called van de Hulst (or anomalous diffraction) approximation was obtained from physical ideas.

Perelman (1979) mathematically deduced another approximation for optically soft particles (*S-approximation*, SA). It is based on the asymptotic behaviour of the Mie series when $m \to 1$. The extinction efficiency factor can be written as follows:

$$Q_{\text{ext}}^{\text{SA}}(m, x) = \frac{1}{2|m|}\text{Re}\left[(m^2 + 1)^2 + \frac{\omega(m, \rho) - \omega(-m, \tilde{R})}{2m}\right], \qquad (2.68)$$

where $\rho = 2(m - 1)x$, $\tilde{R} = 2(m + 1)x$ and

$$\omega(m, z) = \left[a(m) + \frac{a_0(m)}{z^2}\right]\text{ei}(z) +$$

$$ia_1(m)\frac{\exp(-iz)}{z} + a_2(m)\frac{1 - \exp(-iz)}{z^2}.$$

Here

$$\text{ei}(z) = \int_0^z \frac{1 - \exp(-it)}{t}\,\text{d}t$$

is the integral exponential function and the coefficients depend on the refractive index only

$$\begin{cases} a(m) = (m^2 - 1)^2(m^2 + 1) \\ a_0(m) = -2(m^2 - 1)^2(m - 1)^2 \\ a_1(m) = (m + 1)^2(m^4 - 2m^3 - 2m^2 - 2m + 1) \\ a_2(m) = -a_0(m) - a_1(m). \end{cases}$$

The applicability of the S-approximation has essentially been extended by Perelman and Voshchinnikov (2002a, 2002b) both for dielectric and absorbing particles. The expression for the improved S-approximation (ISA) has the following form:

$$Q_{\text{ext}}^{\text{ISA}}(m, x) = \tilde{g}(m, x) Q_{\text{ext}}^{\text{SA}}(m, x), \tag{2.69}$$

where the function $\tilde{g}(m, x)$ is represented as

$$\tilde{g}(m, x) = 1 - \frac{\mathcal{S}(m) - 2}{\mathcal{S}(m)} \tilde{f}(m, x) \tag{2.70}$$

with

$$\mathcal{S}(m) = \lim_{x \to \infty} Q_{\text{ext}}^{\text{SA}}(m, x). \tag{2.71}$$

We have

$$\mathcal{S}(m) = \frac{1}{2|m|} \text{Re} \left[(m^2 + 1)^2 + \frac{(m^2 + 1)(m^2 - 1)^2}{2m} \ln \frac{m - 1}{m + 1} \right]. \tag{2.72}$$

The choice of the smoothing function $\tilde{g}(m, x)$ in Eq. (2.69) is determined by the short wavelength approximation of the extinction factors

$$\lim_{x \to \infty} Q_{\text{ext}}(m, x) = 2. \tag{2.73}$$

By virtue of Eqs. (2.69)–(2.73) the condition

$$\lim_{x \to \infty} \tilde{f}(m, x) = 1$$

has to be satisfied. The function $\tilde{f}(m, x)$ was chosen in the form

$$\tilde{f}(m, x) = \exp \left[-\frac{2.9 \left(1 - 8 \, \text{Im}(m) \right) \exp(4|m|)}{|m|^{11} x} \right]. \tag{2.74}$$

The improved version of the S-approximation describes the behaviour of Mie curves for particles with the real part of refractive indices up to 2.0 or more fairly well (see Fig. 11). It can also be used for absorbing particles with k up to 0.5 (Fig. 12). This approximation may be useful in getting the analytical form of the "smoothed" Mie curves when the ripple-type fluctuations were averaged.

A detailed description of other approximations can be found in the book of Kokhanovsky (1999) and the review of A.R. Jones (1999) (see also Muinonen, 2002).

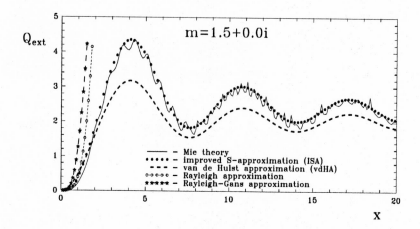

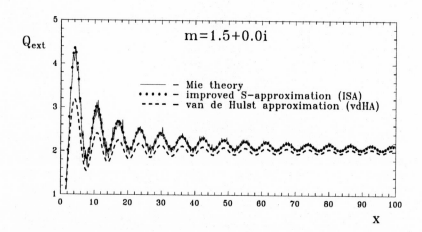

Figure 11 Extinction efficiencies calculated on the basis of the Mie theory, the improved S-approximation (Eq. (2.69)), the van de Hulst approximation (Eq. (2.67)), the Rayleigh and the Rayleigh–Gans approximations. The lower panel has another horizontal scale. Adapted from Perelman and Voshchinnikov (2002a).

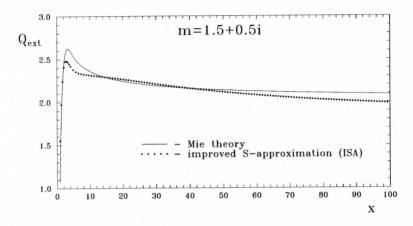

Figure 12 Extinction efficiencies calculated on the basis of the Mie theory and the improved S-approximation (Eq. (2.69)) for absorbing particles. Adapted from Perelman and Voshchinnikov (2002b).

2.2.5   Experiments

Evidently, it is impossible to solve all light scattering problems theoretically because theory considers only a model of particles and has restrictions on particle size, shape, structure, surface roughness. The gaps in theory can be filled in by *experimental techniques*. In this case, a significant advantage is that fewer assumptions or simplifications need to be made. In principle, the measurements of all light scattering characteristics can be performed for a nearly arbitrary particle, which is very important for the study of natural samples like meteoritic dust. However, in practice the experiments have their own *defects* connected with preparation of the samples, restricted dynamical range of the measurement process, frequent impossibility to make the measurements at all scattering angles, etc. Another difficulty is the necessity of developing complex and expensive hardware that leads to the dearth of experimental data.

In principle, experimental results can substitute the theoretical ones. Historically, this dominated in the pre-computer era. At present, the experimental techniques rather help to test (and extend) the results of complicated calculations.

There are two experimental approaches to determine the optical properties of particles, namely *measurements at optical wavelengths* and in *microwave analog experiments*.

Measurements at optical wavelengths.   Modern visible and infrared measurements are performed with a laser as a source of polarized light. They allow one to determine the full scattering matrix for particles (hydrosoles or aerosols) with sizes ranging from several hundredths of a micrometer to several hundred micrometers. Unfortunately, the technical problems preclude measurements in forward and backward directions (i.e. near the scattering angles $\Theta = 0°$ and $180°$). Also the problem with production of small particles of shape and structure well determined beforehand restricts the direct comparison of the theory with experiments. A laboratory technique for optical measurements of scattering matrices for small planetary particles is described by Hovenier (2000) and Volten (2001). Various instruments and methods used in industry and research laboratories are discussed by Bayvel and Jones (1981). Mishchenko *et al.* (2000b) give a short overview of early and recent scattering measurements in different scientific fields. Based on the ground (Hovenier *et al.*, 2003) and microgravity (PROGRA$^{2(10)}$; Hadamcik *et al.*, 2003) experiments, the databases containing the measured scattering matrices for natural, mineral, meteoritic, etc. particles have been created[11].

Microwave analog experiments.   The main idea of this approach is to make the measurements at millimeter or centimeter wavelengths with targets of corresponding sizes based on the fact that the particle optical properties are determined by the ratio of the particle size to the wavelength (see Sect. 2.2.3). Such a scaling of scatterers by a factor of 10^4 to 10^5 has the *advantage* of precisely manufactured targets with well controlled size, shape and refractive index. The particle orientation relative to the incident beam is also known and may be changed during the measuring process. At the same time, the

---

[10] PROGRA^2 — PRopepriétés Optiques des GRains Astronomiques et Atmosphériques.

[11] See the Internet address in Sect. 5.2.

problem is to search for analog materials with optical constants at microwaves close to those of cosmic dust analogues at optical wavelengths.

The pioneering microwave experiments were performed by Greenberg *et al.* (1961; see also Greenberg, 1968). Other results obtained by the microwave technique were presented by Zerull and Giese (1974) and Schuerman (1980). The current state of the method and its recent achievements are described by Gustafson (1996, 2000), Kolokolova and Gustafson (2001) and Gustafson *et al.*. (2001).

2.2.6   WWW database of optical properties

The availability of an electronic database containing as benchmarks various cross-sections, scattering matrices, etc. obtained for particles by experimental and theoretical methods is important not only for astronomy but also for other fields of science. Such a Database of optical properties of cosmic dust analogues (DOP) is now constructed. It considers:

- theoretical aspects — definitions of the optical characteristics of non-spherical scatterers, scatterer models, exact and approximate methods of light scattering theory, light scattering experiments, bibliography of light scattering works;

- application aspects — optical constants of materials, light scattering codes, benchmark results, a graphic library of the optical properties, self-training algorithm for calculation of the optical properties of fractal-like aggregates;

- related resources — radiative transfer tools, miscellaneous aspects.

The database is accessible via the Internet (see the address in Sect. 5.2 and its description is given by Il'in *et al.*, 2003).

2.3   Skill of cooking

2.3.1   Objects' models

Even first-class provision and ideal equipment do not guarantée acceptable quality of the dish, provided the cook's experience is not large enough. In the modelling of dusty objects this means a proper selection not only of optical constants and a light scattering approach but also a model of the object. It includes an appropriate choice of the spatial distribution of scatterers (dust grains) and illuminating sources and correct treatment of radiative transfer effects.

The geometry of an object and the density distribution of grains inside or around it as well as temporal and spatial variations of dust properties are mainly related to the nature of the object and general rules may hardly help.

At the same time, the radiative transfer methods are rather conservative and their changes or modifications usually require huge efforts. As a result, the *radiative transfer code available determines the final result of modelling* but different radiative transfer codes may give different results. During the long history, the radiative transfer theory passed several stages: analytical, semi-analytical and numerical ones. The problems which can be solved analytically are very simple ones like the fluxes from a sphere found in the Eddington approximation assuming the grey opacity and the spherical phase function. Modern observational techniques give the spectral energy distributions, images and polarization maps of very complicated objects like fragmented molecular cloud cores, circumbinary and circumstellar disks. These data cannot be modeled without very complicated radiative transfer programs, and consideration of polarization usually requires application of the Monte Carlo method.

2.3.2   Radiative transfer programs

In order to solve the radiative transfer problem, the following optical properties of dust grains must be defined beforehand:

- extinction cross-sections (see Eq. (2.32)) for calculations of the optical distance inside a dusty object;

- particle albedo (Eq. (2.34)) and the scattering matrix (Eq. (2.25)) for description of the process of light scattering if the polarization is considered or phase function (Eq. (2.31)) if not (in some cases only the asymmetry parameter g (Eq. (2.36)) is used);

- absorption cross-sections which are used for calculations of dust temperature and emitted radiation.

Table 8 contains some characteristics of radiative transfer programs created during the last 25 years and their applications to the interpretation of observed data on dusty cosmic objects. As usual, many modern radiative transfer codes are modifications of earlier versions created at the same institute or university. We do not intend to search for the origin and roots of codes and just note that the author of the original code used to appear as the co-author of further publications. The major part of the papers mentioned in Table 8 are based on two methods: a) iterative scheme to solve the moment equations of radiative transfer equation (methods of moments, MoM) which was originally formulated by Hummer and Rybicki (1971) for spherical geometry with a central point source (1D geometry) and b) Monte Carlo (MC) simulation. In some cases, for simplification of calculations the phase function $\mathcal{F}$ (Eq. (2.31)) is taken in an approximate form suggested by Henyey and Greenstein (1941; HG function, see discussion in Part II, Sect. 6). The standard applications include: circumstellar (CS) shells and envelopes around early (pre-main-sequence; PMS) and late-type stars and young stellar objects (YSO), reflection nebulae (RN), interstellar clouds and globules, diffuse galactic light (DGL) and in recent years galaxies and active galactic nuclei (AGN).

Table 8 Papers presenting new approaches and schemes in radiative transfer in dusty media.

Author(s)	Method; particles; geometry; output; applications
Leung (1976)	MoM, quasi-diffusion approximation; homogeneous and coated spheres; 1D (sphere); intensity, SED; dust clouds with central source, CS shells
Witt (1977)	MC; spheres, HG phase function; plane-parallel layer; intensity; RN

Table 8 (continued).

Author(s)	Method; particles; geometry; output; applications
White (1979)	Doubling method; MRN mixture; homogeneous layer (optically thick but geometrically thin); intensity, polarization; RN
Daniel (1980)	MC; single size spheres; homogeneous sphere; polarization; cool stars
Yorke (1980)	MoM; single size spheres; 1D (sphere), isotropic scattering; SED; cocoon stars
Rowan-Robinson (1980)	Ray tracing method; single size homogeneous and coated spheres; 1D (inhomogeneous sphere), isotropic scattering; SED, intensity profiles; hot-centred interstellar clouds; M giants and supergiants
Lefèvre *et al.* (1982)	MC; graphite and silicate spheres; inhomogeneous sphere, anisotropic scattering; SED; late-type stars
Lefèvre *et al.* (1983)	MC; graphite and silicate spheres; homogeneous ellipsoid, anisotropic scattering; SED, images; young and late-type stars
Warren-Smith (1983)	MC; spheres of different sizes; plane layers; surface brightness, polarization; RN
Spagna and Leung (1983)	Newton–Raphson iterative scheme; spheres (up to 5 constituents); 1D (homogeneous sphere); SED; CS shells, interstellar clouds
Rogers and Martin (1986)	Half-range MoM; spheres; 1D (sphere) with power density distribution; SED; CS shells (IRC +10 216)
Chini *et al.* (1986)	MoM; MRN mixture; 1D (sphere) with power density distribution; SED; CS shells
Wolfire and Cassinelli (1986)	Modified MoM; MRN mixture; 1D (sphere) with power density distribution; SED; protostars
Spagna and Leung (1987)	MoM, quasi-diffusion approximation; homogeneous and coated spheres; 2D (disks); intensity,

Table 8 (continued).

Author(s)	Method; particles; geometry; output; applications
	SED; disk dust clouds; CS disks; disk galaxies
Bastien and Ménard (1988)	MC; spheres; 3D, arbitrary geometry, inhomogeneous density distribution; images, polarization maps; YSO, CS shells
Egan *et al.* (1988)	Updated and comprehensive versions of codes of Leung (1976) and Spagna and Leung (1983) for one-dimensional geometries (sphere, plane-parallel, cylindrical)
Efstathiou and Rowan-Robinson (1990)	Ray tracing method; single and multi-component mixtures of spheres; 2D axisymmetric inhomogeneous configurations (disks, ellipsoids, tori); SED; late type stars, AGN
Höfflich (1991)	MC; Thomson scattering; axisymmetric photospheres; polarization; SN 1987A
Collison and Fix (1991)	Iterative scheme; single size silicate spheres; 2D axisymmetric inhomogeneous shells, isotropic scattering; SED, images; CS shells
Whitney and Hartmann (1992)	MC; spheres, HG phase function; 3D (disks); images, polarization maps; PMS objects
Pier and Krolik (1992)	Multi-dimensional Newton–Raphson technique; MRN mixture; 2D (homogeneous torus); SED; AGN, Seyfert galaxies
Bosma (1993a, 1993b)	New iterative scheme in MoM; anisotropic scattering, randomly oriented particles; 1D (sphere); intensity and polarization;
Fischer (1993)	MC; MRN mixture; 3D, arbitrary geometry, inhomogeneous density distribution; images, polarization maps; protostellar sources
Groenewegen (1993)	Iterative scheme; spheres; 1D (sphere) with power density distribution, isotropic scattering, determination of inner radius as dust condensation boundary; SED; shells around AGB stars

Table 8 (continued).

Author(s)	Method; particles; geometry; output; applications
Voshchinnikov and Karjukin (1994)	MC, method of symmetrized trajectories; spheres (Rayleigh, MRN mixture); 2D (inhomogeneous spheroid); intensity, polarization; CS shells around young stars
Code and Whitney (1995)	MC; electrons, spherical particles; 3D (illuminated spherical blobs); intensity, polarization; supergiants, RCB stars, DGL, RN
Sonnhalter *et al.* (1995)	Frequency dependent flux-limited diffusion approximation; mixture of carbon, silicate and silicate-ice spheres; 2D axially-symmetric dusty disks with different density distribution; intensities, images at different wavelengths
Lopez *et al.* (1995)	MC; carbon spheres; inhomogeneous axisymmetric shell, anisotropic scattering; SED, images; AGB stars, Red Rectangle
Men'shchikov and Henning (1997)	MoM; spheres of different sizes and materials; 2D axially-symmetric CS disks with arbitrary density distribution; SED, images; CS shells, YSO
Ivezić and Elitzur (1997)	Numerical integration; spheres (6 types of materials and 2 size distributions); 1D (sphere and plane-parallel slab); SED; CS shells, interstellar clouds, YSO
Városi and Dwek (1999)	Analytical approximation and MC; spheres; spherically-symmetric two-phase clumpy medium; fluxes; star-forming regions, starburst galaxies
Wolf and Henning (2000); Wolf (2003)	MC including calculations of dust temperature; spheres of different sizes and materials; 3D, arbitrary number, shape and geometrical configuration of illuminating sources and dust density distribution; SED, images, polarization maps; CS shells, AGB stars, YSO, AGN

Table 8 (continued).

Author(s)	Method; particles; geometry; output; applications
Dullemond and Turolla (2000); van Bemmel and Dullemond (2003);	Method of short characteristics in spherical coordinates; spheres of different sizes and materials; 2D axially-symmetric CS envelopes and disks with arbitrary density distribution; SED, colours, images; CS shells, AGN
Gordon et al. (2001); Misselt et al. (2001)	MC; mixture of carbonaceous and silicate grains, polycyclic aromatic hydrocarbons (PAHs); 3D, arbitrary distribution of stars and dust; SED, images, polarization maps; RN, clusters of stars, galaxies
Wolf et al. (2002)	Dissemination of MC code of Wolf and Henning (2000) on non-spherical particles
Moreno et al. (2002)	MC; experimental scattering matrices; spherical shell around spherical nucleus; input/output radiation, fluxes, polarization; comets
Whitney and Wolff (2002)	Dissemination of MC codes of Whitney and Hartmann (1992) and Code and Whitney (1995) on non-spherical particles
Hegmann and Kegel (2003)	Iterative solution to discretized radiative transfer equation; spheres, HG phase function; 1D configuration (plane–parallel slab, sphere) with stochastic density distribution; intensity; interstellar clouds
Ueta and Meixner (2003)	Method of long characteristics in axisymmetric system; spheres, modified HG phase function; 2D axially-symmetric CS shells with layered density distribution; SED, images; AGB stars,
Juvela and Padoan (2003)	MC; spheres and PAHs; 3D (illuminated inhomogeneous clouds); IR spectra and images, colours; intensity; interstellar clouds

Table 8 (continued).

Author(s)	Method; particles; geometry; output; applications
Joiner and Leung (2003)	Generalization of the scheme of Leung (1976) on polarization using the technique of Bosma (1993b); single-size AC and silicate spheres; 1D (homogeneous and inhomogeneous sphere with central source and illuminated from outside); flux and polarization of emerging radiation in the near-IR, visible and UV parts of spectrum; CS shells (IRC +10 216)
Niccolini et al. (2003)	Refined version of the code of Lopez et al.(1995);
Lucas (2003)	MC; aligned spheroids; 1D (homogeneous sphere) and 2D (disk + envelope) images, polarization maps; YSO
Steinacker et al. (2003)	Direct solution to discretizated radiative transfer equation; spheres; 3D arbitrary configuration; SED, images; CS shells, YSO, AGN
Stamatellos and Whitworth (2003)	MC; MRN mixture; clouds with spherical inclusions; SED; intensity profiles; molecular clouds with prestellar cores
Gonçalves et al. (2003)	MC; MRN mixture; clouds with non-spherical inclusions; SED; IR images; molecular clouds with prestellar cores

A short description of recent progress in continuum radiative transfer modelling is given in the review of Henning (2001). It is significant that several codes which treat light scattering by aligned non-spherical particles (Wolf et al., 2002; Whitney and Wolff, 2002; Lucas, 2003) appeared in the last few years.

The old and still troublesome problem is verification of numerical codes. It was seriously analyzed by Ivezić et al. (1997) who compared three different radiative transfer codes and obtained the benchmark results for temperature and emerging spectra in the case of spherical geometry.

Note that astronomers can use results and experience gained in other fields of science. For example, 3D radiative transfer codes are widely used in the terrestrial atmosphere applications as described, for example, by Cahalan (2000; see also Sect. 5.2).

2.4 Is it tasty?

The final stage of cooking is tasting — comparison of the characteristics of the prepared food with those expected (existed in mind). In the case of modelling this means the *comparison with available observations*. The coincidence of the model predictions with observations is the best proof of the quality of the cooked dish (chosen model). But before testing a ready fare one needs to manage this process to get the full impression.

2.4.1 *Comparison with observations*

Besides a standard reduction of observational data that is traditionally done by observers, a modeller has to think about the following:

- subtraction of the foreground extinction and polarization or dust emission if a distant object is considered;

- reduction of the infrared fluxes (SEDs) for the beam size;

- correction for blends in the case of dust features.

After this, comparison of the theory with the observations can give full satisfaction like tasting a well cooked dish. However, one needs to remember that similar (or even the same) result can be obtained using other ingredients and that *tastes differ*.

It should also be kept in mind that pleasure may be spoiled if a well-studied object is chosen for modelling because it posses a huge amount of detailed observational information. This situation is characterized as "uncomfortable reality" by Men'shchikov *et al.* (2001) who modeled the observations of the dusty envelope around the carbon star IRC +10 216.

2.4.2   Waste products

After any cooking some waste products always remain. The procedure of modelling of dusty objects also gives something like this. The interaction of radiation and dust is one (and the most "bright") side of dust manifestation in cosmic objects. Other sides include the interaction of dust grains with *gas* and *magnetic fields*. This is related to the *physics* of cosmic dust and connected with the exchange of energy, momentum and charge between gas and dust in the process of their collisions. The corresponding topics are:

- heating of gas by the photoelectric emission from grains;

- heating of grains in coronal gas and shock waves;

- nucleation of dust grains in stellar atmospheres and outflows;

- growth of dust grains by accretion;

- destruction of grains by sputtering;

- radiation pressure, momentum transfer and mass loss in late-type stars;

- molecule formation on grain surfaces;

- the process of grain charging in interstellar clouds and proto-planetary disks;

- the process of non-spherical grain alignment in anisotropic gaseous flows and magnetic fields and disorientation due to collisions with gas particles.

However, treatment of many of the mentioned processes is impossible without the consideration of interaction of radiation and dust (e.g., the photoelectric emission from grains). And in all cases the correctness of the used theory or numerical method is confirmed by the comparison with observations, i.e. again with the *optics of dust grains*.

3 FORWARD, ONLY FORWARD

In the next sections, the *extinction, scattering* and *absorption/emission* properties of dust grains are considered. The connection between the observational phenomena and light scattering theory is shown in Table 9.

Table 9 Observations and light scattering characteristics determined from them.

Phenomena	Light scattering characteristics
Interstellar extinction $A(\lambda)$ (Sect. 3)	Extinction efficiencies Q_{ext}
Interstellar polarization $P(\lambda, \Theta = 0°)$ (Sect. 3)	Polarization efficiencies $(Q_{\text{ext}}^{\text{TM}} - Q_{\text{ext}}^{\text{TE}})$
Scattered radiation $I(\Theta)$ (Part II, Sect. 6)	Albedo Λ and asymmetry factors g or phase function $\mathcal{F}(\Theta)$
Polarization of scattered radiation $P(\Theta)$ (Part II, Sect. 6)	Scattering matrix
IR continuum $F(\lambda)$ (Part II, Sect. 7)	Absorption efficiencies Q_{abs}
IR bands (Part II, Sect. 7)	Extinction (absorption) efficiencies $Q_{\text{ext, (abs)}}$
Dust dynamics (Part II, Sect. 8)	Radiation pressure efficiencies Q_{pr}

3.1 Interstellar extinction: observations

Observational analysis of interstellar extinction was the first research of dust in the Galaxy but it remains relevant and important up to now. Such investigations (as well as other studies of the dust) are performed in two directions: "in depth" and "in breadth". The first way involves examination of the *wavelength dependence of extinction* and gives information about the properties of interstellar grains. The second one includes study of the distribution of dust matter and relates to work on galactic structure.

3.1.1 Extinction curve: general behaviour and variations

The observed wavelength dependence of interstellar extinction (*interstellar extinction curve*) is usually obtained by comparing the brightness of two stars of the same spectral class and luminosity one of which is located behind a dusty cloud and another is not. This "pair method" is applied to early-type stars because of the small number of lines in their spectra. If $m_1(\lambda)$ and $m_2(\lambda)$ are the monochromatic visible stellar magnitudes for stars with extinction and without it, respectively, then

$$m_1(\lambda) = M(\lambda) - 5 + 5\log D_1 + A(\lambda), \qquad (3.1)$$

$$m_2(\lambda) = M(\lambda) - 5 + 5\log D_2, \qquad (3.2)$$

where $M(\lambda)$ is the absolute stellar magnitude and D_1, D_2 are the distances to the stars. The difference of stellar magnitudes is

$$\Delta m(\lambda) \equiv m_1(\lambda) - m_2(\lambda) = A(\lambda) + 5\log(D_1/D_2). \qquad (3.3)$$

The term $5\log(D_1/D_2)$ can be excluded if observations are performed at two wavelengths λ_1 and λ_2 ($\lambda_1 < \lambda_2$)

$$\Delta m(\lambda_1) - \Delta m(\lambda_2) = E(\lambda_1 - \lambda_2) = A(\lambda_1) - A(\lambda_2). \qquad (3.4)$$

The quantity $E(\lambda_1 - \lambda_2)$ is named the *colour excess* of the star behind the dusty cloud. Usually, the colour excess for the photometric bands B and V (effective wavelengths $\lambda_B = 0.44\,\mu m$ and $\lambda_V = 0.55\,\mu m$) is considered and the *normalized extinction curves* are studied

$$A^{(n)}(\lambda^{-1}) \equiv \frac{E(\lambda - V)}{E(B - V)} = \frac{A(\lambda) - A_V}{A_B - A_V} = \frac{\Delta m(\lambda) - \Delta m(V)}{\Delta m(B) - \Delta m(V)}. \qquad (3.5)$$

Here, A_B and A_V is the extinction in the B and V bands, respectively. Sometimes, the normalization of the extinction curve on A_V or extinction in another band is used.

As follows from Eq. (3.4), the pair (or colour difference) method does not give the absolute value of extinction but only the "selective" extinction (*reddening*), i.e. the difference of extinction at two wavelengths. The term "reddening" appeared in the 1940s when the increase of extinction with frequency was definitely established (see the discussion in Sharpless, 1963 and Straižys, 1992).

The absolute value of extinction can be determined through the coefficient converting the selective extinction to A_V. As a rule, it is expressed via the colour excess $E(B - V)$

$$A_V = R_V E(B - V), \qquad (3.6)$$

where the coefficient R_V ($\equiv R_{VB}$) is often evaluated from observations in the visible and IR taking into account that $A_\lambda \to 0$ when $\lambda \to \infty$. From Eq. (3.5), it follows that

$$R_V = \frac{A_V}{E(B - V)} = -\frac{E(\infty - V)}{E(B - V)}. \qquad (3.7)$$

The average value of R_V in our Galaxy lies in the range from 3.0 to 3.2 (Straižys, 1978; Patriarchi *et al.*, 2003; Wegner, 2003). The wide scatter of the published data ($R_V \approx 2.0 - 5.5$) occurs for stars with colour excesses $E(B - V) \lesssim 0^{\rm m}5$ (see Fig. 3 in Patriarchi *et al.*, 2003 and Fig. 4 in Wegner, 2003). It tends to diminish with growing $E(B - V)$ and distance to stars. Here, $R_V = 3.1$ is adopted following Savage and Mathis (1979) and Fitzpatrick (1999). Different methods for the determination of R_V are reviewed by Straižys (1992).

The use of the expression (3.7) suggests that *neutral extinction* in the interstellar medium is absent[12]. The absolute extinction can be estimated from Eq. (3.1) or Eq. (3.3) if the distance to the star is known and the stellar flux has been calculated from the theory of stellar atmospheres. There are also special methods to evaluate R_V which involve the neutral extinction A_0 (Straižys, 1992). Their application showed that the neutral extinction seemed to be negligible in the solar neighbourhood (see also discussion in Whittet, 1992, 2003). However, Skórzyński *et al.* (2003) conclude on the possible presence of a grey (neutral) interstellar extinction for stars with distances up

---

[12] Otherwise it must be added to the nominator of first fraction in (3.7).

to 400 pc. They apply Eq. (3.1) and compare the observed and intrinsic visual absolute stellar magnitudes for 556 O–B3 stars of different luminosity classes. The first magnitudes are found using apparent brightness of stars, their Hipparcos distances and their visual extinction as $R_V E(B - V)$, while the second ones are estimated from the spectral type and luminosity class of stars. It is established that *the first (observed) magnitudes are systematically larger than the second (intrinsic) ones.* This effect is attributed to the neutral extinction whose average value for all considered stars was evaluated as large as $A_0 \approx 1\overset{m}{.}3$ if $R_V = 3.1$ and $A_0 \approx 0\overset{m}{.}84$ if $R_V = 6$. Patriarchi *et al.* (2003) support the presence of the neutral extinction for a few stars of their sample whose Hipparcos parallaxes are reliable. Using 56 O and B stars with most accurately measured trigonometric parallaxes, Skórzyński *et al.* (2003) find that A_0 seems to reach its maximum at distance from 110 to 150 pc. The errors in the determination of neutral extinction are quite large and some extreme values of A_0 can be related to the incorrect Hipparcos distances (see, e.g., Steele *et al.*, 1998), erroneous spectral classification or local (circumstellar) material. Nevertheless, the importance of this phenomenon should not be underestimated. Note also that the "grey" intergalactic dust producing the wavelength-independent extinction is invoked as a possible explanation of the apparent systematic dimming of high-redshift Type Ia supernovae (Aguirre, 1999).

In general, the interstellar extinction curve has a power law-like rise from the IR to the visible, a prominent feature (bump) near λ 2175 Å, and a steep rise in the far-UV. Spectrophotometric observations have discovered a number of diffuse interstellar absorption bands and wide shallow features (very broad structure) in the visible part of spectrum, while the attempts to detect the absorption features in the UV have failed (Clayton *et al.*, 2003a). Figure 13 shows the mean galactic extinction curve plotted using the approximation of Fitzpatrick (1999; see Sect. 3.1.2). In the near IR-visible part of the spectrum, the distinction between the extinction curves of different stars is rather small although essential variations of the curve for stars in Cygnus, Perseus and Cassiopea (a "knee" near $\lambda^{-1} = 2.3\,\mu m^{-1}$) is known for a long time (Nandy, 1966).

In the UV, extinction curves differ strongly (Fig. 14). The Figure demonstrates the enormous range of properties exhibited by the UV

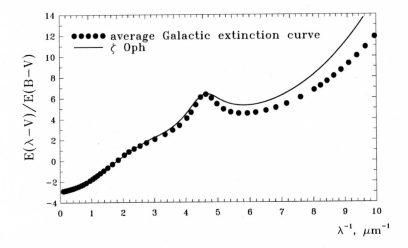

Figure 13 The average galactic extinction curve (according to Fitzpatrick, 1999; see also Table 10) and the extinction curve in the direction of ζ Oph (Fitzpatrick and Massa, 1990; Serkowski *et al.*, 1975).

extinction in the Milky Way and that the mean curve in the UV obviously has little meaning.

As follows from observations at the satellites IUE and TD-1a (Gürtler *et al.*, 1982; Fitzpatrick and Massa, 1986), the profile of the bump is symmetric. The position of its center varies a little from star to star and occurs at $\lambda_0 = 2174 \pm 17\,\text{Å}$ or $\lambda_0^{-1} = 4.599 \pm 0.012\,\mu\text{m}^{-1}$ (Fitzpatrick and Massa, 1986). The largest deviations from this value were found for stars HD 50083 and HD 6273 ($\lambda_0 = 2110\,\text{Å}$, $\lambda_0^{-1} = 4.74\,\mu\text{m}^{-1}$) and for stars HD 45321 and HD 69080 ($\lambda_0 = 2270\,\text{Å}$, $\lambda_0^{-1} = 4.40\,\mu\text{m}^{-1}$) (Friedemann and Gürtler, 1986).

The total half-width of the bump is $W = 0.992 \pm 0.058\,\mu\text{m}^{-1}$ that corresponds to $470 \pm 27\,\text{Å}$. Variations of W are sufficiently large; values of W lie between $W = 0.768\,\mu\text{m}^{-1}$ (360 Å) for HD 93028 (Fitzpatrick and Massa, 1986) and $W = 1.62\,\mu\text{m}^{-1}$ (720 Å) for HD 29647 (Cardelli and Savage, 1988). A correlation between λ_0 and W was not found, but the width of the feature $\lambda 2175\,\text{Å}$ was revealed to be greater for stars located in dark clouds.

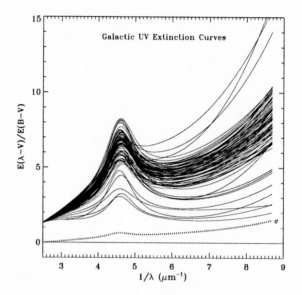

Figure 14 UV extinction curves for 80 galactic stars derived from International Ultraviolet Explorer (IUE) satellite observations. The observational data were fitted using the analytical expressions derived by Fitzpatrick and Massa (1990). After Fitzpatrick (1999).

3.1.2 Extinction curve: fitting

Dorschner (1973) was the first who suggested to approximate the shape of the bump profile by the classical (Lorentzian) dispersion profile. The analytical formula for the representation of the extinction curve including the bump was proposed by Seaton (1979). After examination of the IUE extinction curves for many lines of sight, Fitzpatrick and Massa (1986, 1990) deduced a single analytical expression with a small number of parameters for the representation of the UV extinction (see Eq. (3.10)).

Cardelli *et al.* (1989) discovered that the shape of the UV extinction curves correlated with the parameter R_V. This suggests that the

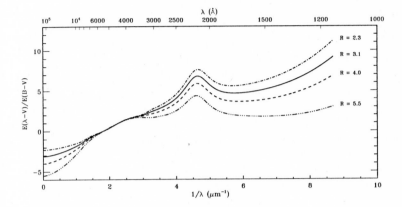

Figure 15 Far-IR through UV extinction curves from Cardelli *et al.* (1989). The curves were approximated as a one-parameter family that varied linearly with R_V^{-1} (Eq. (3.8)). After Fitzpatrick (1999).

extinction curves from the UV through the IR can be characterized as approximately a one-parameter family dependent on R_V (Fig. 15). In this Figure, four representative extinction curves are shown, each determined by the value of R_V listed at the right-hand side of the curves. According to Cardelli *et al.* (1989), the normalized extinction curves in the range $\lambda^{-1} = 0.3$–$8\,\mu m^{-1}$ can be described by the dependence

$$A(\lambda)/A_V = \tilde{a}(\lambda^{-1}) + \tilde{b}(\lambda^{-1})/R_V, \qquad (3.8)$$

with the polynomial coefficients $\tilde{a}(\lambda^{-1})$ and $\tilde{b}(\lambda^{-1})$, where λ^{-1} is in units μm^{-1}. Later, O'Donnell (1994) revised these coefficients at the optical and near UV wavelengths $(0.3\,\mu m^{-1} \leq \lambda^{-1} \leq 3.3\,\mu m^{-1})$.

The IR extinction was analyzed by Martin and Whittet (1990) who approximated the extinction at wavelengths $\lambda = 0.7$–$5\,\mu m$ as follows:

$$\frac{A(\lambda)}{E(B-V)} = \lambda^{-1.84}. \qquad (3.9)$$

Due to such uniform wavelength dependence of the interstellar extinction at large wavelengths, the IR colour excesses can be applied for the determination of the total extinction (see Sect. 3.1.3).

Fitzpatrick (1999; see also Fitzpatrick, 2004) derived a new wavelength dependence of the average galactic extinction curve from the IR through the UV. He rejected the use of the pair method because of its overestimation of the monochromatic extinction in the vicinity of λ_{eff} for early-type stars. In order to find the optical/IR extinction, the synthetic photometry of an artificially reddened stellar energy distribution was compared with that of an identical but unreddened star. The stellar energy distribution was calculated using the models of stellar atmospheres. Later, comparison with observations was performed to improve the fitting. The adopted extinction for Johnson and Strömgren photometric bands is given in Table 2 of Fitzpatrick (1999). In the UV region ($1150\,\text{Å} \leq \lambda < 2700\,\text{Å}$), the following expressions can be applied ($y \equiv \lambda^{-1}$)

$$A^{(n)}(y) = \frac{E(\lambda - V)}{E(B - V)} = c_1 + c_2 y + c_3 D(y, W, y_0) + c_4 \tilde{F}(y), \quad (3.10)$$

where

$$c_2 = -0.824 + 4.717 \times R_V^{-1}, \quad (3.11)$$

$$c_1 = 2.030 - 3.007 \times c_2, \quad (3.12)$$

$$D(y, W, y_0) = \frac{y^2}{(y^2 - y_0^2)^2 + y^2 W^2} \quad (3.13)$$

and

$$\begin{cases} \tilde{F}(y) = 0.5392(y - 5.9)^2 + 0.05644(y - 5.9)^3, \\ \qquad\qquad\qquad\qquad \text{for } y \geq 5.9\,\mu\text{m}^{-1}, \\ \tilde{F}(y) = 0, \qquad\qquad\qquad \text{for } y < 5.9\,\mu\text{m}^{-1}. \end{cases} \quad (3.14)$$

Equations (3.10), (3.13) and (3.14) were suggested by Fitzpatrick and Massa (1990), while the R_V-dependence of the coefficients c_1 and c_2 (Eqs. (3.11), (3.12)) was introduced by Fitzpatrick (1999). Equation (3.10) consists of: *i*) a Lorentzian-like bump term (requiring three parameters, corresponding to the bump width W, position y_0, and strength c_3), *ii*) a far-UV curvature term (one parameter c_4), and *iii*) a linear term underlying the bump and the far-UV (two parameters c_1 and c_2). This set of basis functions is illustrated in Fig. 16. With the proper choice of these six parameters, practically all UV

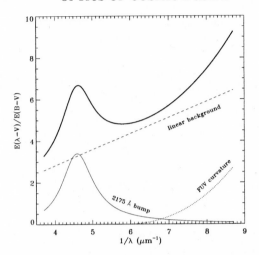

Figure 16 Analytical fitting functions for UV extinction curves from Fitzpatrick and Massa (1990). A normalized UV extinction curve (thick solid curve) can be represented by a combination of three functions: *i*) a linear background component (thin dashed line), *ii*) a UV bump component (thin solid curve), and *iii*) a far-UV curvature component (thin dotted line). Parameterized functions are given by Eqs. (3.10)–(3.14). After Fitzpatrick (1999).

extinction curves can be reproduced to within uncertainties inherent in the data. For most sightlines, the number of free parameters can be reduced to four, since the position of the 2175 Å bump is nearly invariant and the intercept and slope of the linear term are tightly correlated. Values of the coefficients specifying the mean galactic extinction curve are given in Table 10. For 78 stars observed from IUE, the coefficients were derived by Fitzpatrick and Massa (1990). Jenniskens and Greenberg (1993) estimated the coefficients $c_1, ..., c_4$ for 115 stars. A series of the R_V-dependent curves recommended for dereddening of the photometric data was calculated by Fitzpatrick and can be obtained via anonymous ftp (see Sect. 5.2).

For the far UV wavelength region ($920\,\text{Å} \leq \lambda < 1180\,\text{Å}$), Sasseen *et al.* (2002) suggested the following dependence for a mean galactic extinction curve

$$\frac{E(\lambda - V)}{E(B - V)} = d_0 + d_1 y + d_2 y^2, \qquad (3.15)$$

where the coefficients are: $d_0 = 34.78$, $d_1 = -7.929$ and $d_2 = 0.5554$. The dependence (3.15) is based on the best measurements of the extiction curve for seven stars which spectra were obtained with the Berkeley extreme UV/far UV spectrometer during two ORFEUS[13] missions.

3.1.3 Absolute extinction: determination from infrared colour excesses

The use of Eq. (3.6) to evaluate the interstellar extinction in a selected direction is embarrassed by the choice of the value of R_V. It can be evaluated from observations in the B, V bands and in an IR band (say a X band)

$$R_V = R_{VX} \frac{E(V - X)}{E(B - V)}, \qquad (3.16)$$

where the coefficient R_{VX} is analogous to R_V and converts the selective extinction to the total one

$$R_{VX} = \frac{A_V}{A_V - A_X}. \qquad (3.17)$$

For a long time, the coefficients R_{VX} were chosen in an arbitrary manner so as to conform to van de Hulst's theoretical curve N 15 (see Johnson, 1968). Later, IR observations settled down. A recent determination of the coefficients was made by Fitzpatrick (1999) who suggested the following values:

$$R_{VJ} = 1.39, \quad R_{VH} = 1.19, \quad R_{VK} = 1.12, \quad R_{VL} = 1.07. \qquad (3.18)$$

---

[13] ORFEUS — Orbiting and Retrievable Far and Extreme Ultraviolet Spectrometers.

Fitzpatrick (1999) notes that these coefficients actually depend on the value of $E(B - V)$ but vary by only a few hundredths in the range $E(B - V) = 0^m0-2^m0$. Near IR colour excesses (in particular, the colour excess $E(H - K)$) can be used for estimating A_V of objects observed through dark clouds (see discussion in Teixeira and Emerson, 1999 and references therein).

A theoretical consideration of the coefficients R_{VX} was made by Voshchinnikov and Il'in (1987). They calculated the coefficients for core-mantle cylindrical grains and analyzed previous calculations for spherical grains. The conclusion is that for the J, H, K bands the coefficients reflect a general behaviour of light scattering by small particles and are insensitive to the chemical composition, grain shape and structure, etc. The following coefficients were recommended:

$$R_{VJ} = 1.38, \quad R_{VH} = 1.20, \quad R_{VK} = 1.12. \qquad (3.19)$$

The excellent coincidence of the theoretical (Eq. (3.19)) and empirical (Eq. (3.18)) coefficients demonstrates their reliability.

Frequently, it is difficult to evaluate the extinction in the V band for highly obscured objects. Then the colour excess in any pair of bands X, Y (other than the V band) can be used. The expression for the coefficient R_{XY} can easily be obtained in terms of the coefficients R_{VX}, R_{VY}:

$$R_{XY} = \frac{(R_{VX} - 1)R_{VY}}{R_{VX} - R_{VY}}. \qquad (3.20)$$

3.1.4   Extinction in diffuse interstellar medium: from infrared to X-rays

Observations in the far-UV show that the growth of the interstellar extinction continues almost up to the Lyman limit (Snow *et al.*, 1990; Sasseen *et al.*, 2002). At wavelengths shorter than 912 Å, the extinction is dominated by photoionization of atoms but not by the scattering and absorption by dust. In the extreme UV ($\lambda\,100-912\,\text{Å}$), almost all radiation from distant objects is "consumed" by neutral hydrogen and helium in the close vicinity of the Sun. In the X-range, photoionization of other abundant atoms (C, N, O, etc.) becomes important. However, the presence of ionized gas in some directions (e.g., H II regions) makes the interstellar medium transparent up to very large distances and even extragalactic sources can be observed at $\lambda \sim 100\,\text{Å}$ (Bowyer *et al.*, 2000).

In order to consider extinction in a very wide spectral range, it is convenient to convert $A(\lambda)$ in stellar magnitudes to extinction cross-sections $\sigma_{\text{d}}(\lambda)$ related to column density of H-atoms. This procedure is described by the following expression:

$$\sigma_{\text{d}}(\lambda) = \frac{A(\lambda)}{1.086\,N(\text{H})} = \frac{R_V}{1.086} \left[\frac{N(\text{H})}{E(\text{B}-\text{V})}\right]^{-1} \left[1 + \frac{A^{(n)}(\lambda)}{R_V}\right],$$
(3.21)

where the normalized extinction is given by Eq. (3.5) and the ratio of the hydrogen column density to the colour excess $N(\text{H})/E(\text{B}-\text{V})$ (i.e. the gas to dust ratio) can be found from observations taking into account neutral, molecular and ionized hydrogen. The results of the determination of the ratio $N(\text{HI})/E(\text{B}-\text{V})$ were summarized by Burnashev (1999) (see also Vuong *et al.*, 2003). Ryter (1996) deduced the ratio

$$\frac{N(\text{H})}{E(\text{B}-\text{V})} = 6.83 \times 10^{21} \text{ atoms cm}^{-2}\,\text{mag}^{-1},$$
(3.22)

where the contribution to this value of HI, H_2 and n_e (ionized hydrogen) is 72%, 24% and 4%, respectively. Using this ratio and $R_V = 3.1$, we get from Eq. (3.21)

$$\sigma_{\text{d}}(\lambda) = 4.18 \times 10^{-22} \left[1 + \frac{A^{(n)}(\lambda)}{3.1}\right] = 4.18 \times 10^{-22}\,\frac{A(\lambda)}{A_V}.$$
(3.23)

In the extreme UV, the extinction cross-sections depend on the gas ionization degree and can be approximated as follows:

$$\sigma_{\text{g}}(\lambda) \approx \frac{N(\text{HI})}{N(\text{H})}\,k_{\text{HI}} \left(\frac{\lambda}{912\,\text{Å}}\right)^3 + \frac{N(\text{HeI})}{N(\text{H})}\,k_{\text{HeI}} \left(\frac{\lambda}{504\,\text{Å}}\right)^2,$$
(3.24)

where $k_{\text{HI}} = 6.30 \times 10^{-18}\,\text{cm}^2$ and $k_{\text{HeI}} = 7.83 \times 10^{-18}\,\text{cm}^2$ are the absorption coefficients near the Lyman limit per hydrogen and helium atom, respectively. The first term in Eq. (3.24) differs from zero at $\lambda \leq 912\,\text{Å}$ and the second one does at $\lambda \leq 504\,\text{Å}$. More exact approximations of the photoionization cross-sections of various atoms can be found in Kholtygin *et al.* (1997).

Absorption by molecular hydrogen is rather small in the diffuse interstellar medium and can be neglected (Snow *et al.*, 1990; Wilms *et al.*, 2000).

In the X-ray range ($E = 0.25$–$10\,\text{keV}$ or $\lambda = 0.000124$–$0.005\,\mu\text{m}$ or $\lambda = 1.24$–$50\,\text{Å}$), simplified expressions from Ryter (1996) can be used. He approximated a set of the values given by Morrison and McCammon (1983) in the following way:

$$
\sigma_{\text{g}}(E) = \begin{cases}
110.52 \times 10^{-24} E^{-2.7235}, \\
\quad \text{for } 0.250\,\text{keV} \leq E < 0.532\,\text{keV}, \\
(243.88 \times 10^{-24} - 16.594 \times 10^{-24} E) E^{-2.3480}, \\
\quad \text{for } 0.532\,\text{keV} \leq E < 7.111\,\text{keV}, \\
436.84 \times 10^{-24} E^{-2.6617}, \\
\quad \text{for } 7.111\,\text{keV} \leq E \leq 10.0\,\text{keV},
\end{cases}
$$
$$(3.25)$$

where $\sigma_{\text{g}}(E)$ is in cm^2 and E in keV ($\lambda[\mu\text{m}] = 1.240 \times 10^{-3}/E[\text{keV}]$). Absorption of X-rays in the interstellar medium in the energy range $E = 0.1$–$10\,\text{keV}$ was recently considered by Wilms *et al.* (2000) who used updated photoionization cross-sections and the cosmic abundances of Snow and Witt (1996).

Voshchinnikov and Il'in (1993) calculated the extinction curves in the extreme UV and found that absorption by dust becomes comparable with that of gas at $\lambda \lesssim 150\,\text{Å}$ if there is a considerable fraction of small particles in the interstellar medium and/or the dust to gas ratio is higher than the average one.

The resulting wavelength dependence of extinction in the diffuse interstellar medium is plotted in Fig. 17. The sources of the data are collected in Table 10.

Note that the gas to dust ratio in dense clouds can be determined using the hydrogen column density obtained from X-ray absorption and the near IR extinction. It was firstly made by Vuong *et al.* (2003) who investigated the X-ray spectra of T Tauri stars without accretion disks. For the ρ Oph cloud and old solar abundances (see Sect. 2.1.1)

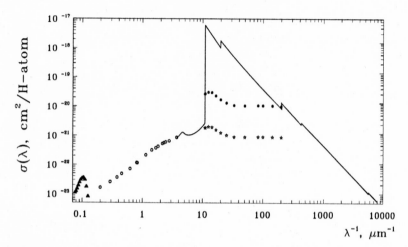

Figure 17 Extinction in the diffuse interstellar medium. The sources of the data are given in Table 10.

it was obtained

$$\frac{N_{\rm X}({\rm H})}{A_{\rm J}} \approx 5.6 \times 10^{21} \text{ atoms cm}^{-2} \text{ mag}^{-1}. \qquad (3.26)$$

Using the value $R_{\rm V} = 3.1$ and Eq. (3.19), we find

$$\frac{N_{\rm X}({\rm H})}{E({\rm B} - {\rm V})} \approx 4.8 \times 10^{21} \text{ atoms cm}^{-2} \text{ mag}^{-1}. \qquad (3.27)$$

This value is smaller than the standard gas to dust ratio given by Eq. (3.22) but exceeds the ratios cited in Table 10.

3.1.5 Large-scale extinction in the Galaxy

The galactic distribution of dust is usually studied from star counts in the visible part of spectrum. The distribution of the visual extinction $A_{\rm V}$ perpendicular to the galactic plane is well described by the barometric law deduced by Parenago (1940)

$$A_{\rm V} = \frac{a_{\rm V} z_{\rm d}}{|\sin b|} \left(1 - e^{-(D|\sin b|/z_{\rm d})}\right), \qquad (3.28)$$

Table 10 Sources of data for extinction in the interstellar medium $\sigma(\lambda)$ presented in Fig. 17.

	Wavelengths	Source
"Silicate" feature	13–8 μm	Table 3* from Rieke and Lebofsky (1985)
Visible	5–0.36 μm	Table 2* from Fitzpatrick (1999)
Ultraviolet	0.27–0.0912 μm	Eqs. (3.10)–(3.14)* with the values from Fitzpatrick (1999)**: y_0 (bump position) = 4.596 μm^{-1}, W(bump width) = 0.99 μm^{-1}, c_3 (bump strength) = 3.23, c_4 (FUV curvature) = 0.41
Extreme UV	0.0912–0.01 μm	Gas: Eq. (3.24) with the values $N(\mathrm{HI})/N(\mathrm{H}) = 0.95$ and $N(\mathrm{HeI})/N(\mathrm{H}) = 0.10$; Dust: calculations of Voshchinnikov and Il'in (1993) for the standard MRN mixture (open circles) and for the case of larger fraction of small particles ($n(r_s) \propto r_s^{-4}$) and the gas to dust ratio $N(\mathrm{H})/E(\mathrm{B}-\mathrm{V}) = 8 \times 10^{20}$ atoms cm^{-2} mag^{-1} (filled circles***)
X-rays	0.005–0.000125 μm	Eq. (3.24) and Eq. (3.25) (approximations from Ryter, 1996)

* Values of $\sigma_d(\lambda)$ were recalculated using Eq. (3.23); ** Far UV extinction obtained from Eq. (3.15) is practically indistinguishable from the extrapolated curve of Fitzpatrick (1999); *** This value was found for the region of dark clouds in Chamaeleon (Whittet et al., 1987) but an even smaller value $N(\mathrm{H})/E(\mathrm{B}-\mathrm{V}) \leq 5 \times 10^{20}$ atoms cm^{-2} mag^{-1} was determined for the local interstellar medium at high galactic altitudes (Knude and Høg, 1999).

where b is the galactic latitude of an obscured object, D the distance to it, a_V the differential extinction (in mag/kpc) in the galactic plane ($b = 0°$), and z_d the extinction scale height. The value of z_d is usually taken to be about 100 pc (Martin, 1978). The quantity a_V has been determined many times (see Burnashev, 1999 for a review).

Unfortunately, Eq. (3.28) displays neither longitude (l) extinction variations nor small-scale variations arising due to dense interstellar clouds. These variations were taken into account in numerous investigations of the distribution of stars and galaxies which gave the extinction as a function of the galactic coordinates and distance $A_V(l, b, D)$. Hakkila et $al.$ (1997) compiled results of these studies in the form of a FORTRAN subroutinewhich calculated A_V and its error for given l, b and $D \leq 5$ kpc. Applications of the computational tool show that up to distances $D \lesssim 1$ kpc the average differential extinction in the galactic plane   is $\langle a_V \rangle = 1\overset{m}{.}5 \pm 0\overset{m}{.}1$ kpc^{-1} and the total extinction towards each galactic pole is $A_V = 0\overset{m}{.}1 \pm 0\overset{m}{.}2$ (Hakkila et $al.$, 1997). This extinction arises almost completely in the interstellar clouds since the intercloud extinction does not exceed $0\overset{m}{.}001 \div 0\overset{m}{.}003$ per 100 pc (Burnashev, 1999). Hakkila et $al.$ (1997) also concluded that studies of the large-scale interstellar extinction in the galactic plane tended to underestimate extinction at distances greater than 1 kpc.

Another possibility to study all-sky extinction distribution appeared after the COBE/DIRBE experiment when observations of the far-IR emission from dust at $\lambda = 100\,\mu$m and $240\,\mu$m were transformed into visual extinction maps (Schlegel et $al.$, 1998[14]). However, testing these maps for a region in the Taurus dark cloud complex made by Arce and Goodman (1999) showed that the maps overestimated extinction by a factor of $1.3 \div 1.5$ for $A_V > 0\overset{m}{.}5$. A larger overestimation of A_V (by a factor $2 \div 3$) in comparison with star counts was found by Cambrésy et $al.$ (2001) in the Polaris molecular cirrus cloud. It is connected with the use of single dust temperature for each line of sight and $\tau_{\text{far-IR}}/A_V$ ratio by Schlegel et $al.$ (1998). Dutra et $al.$ (2003a) performed another calibration of the COBE reddening maps using the colour excesses $E(B - V)$ of the early-type galaxies observed at different galactic latitudes. These colour excesses were

---

[14] The reddening maps are available via Internet (see Sect.5.2).

compared with those determined from 100 μm dust emission. The agreement was found up to $E(B - V) \approx 0^m_.25$. For larger values, the reddening maps of Schlegel *et al.* (1998) give the extinction larger by a factor ~ 1.33.

A three-dimensional galactic extinction model was constructed by Drimmel *et al.* (2003) on the basis of the near IR (J and K bands) and far-IR data from the COBE/DIRBE experiment. This model is capable of rendering extinctions to distances as far as 8 kpc in the galactic plane. The instructions of the method application and example can be found in the Internet (see the address in Sect. 5.2).

An all-sky catalogue of dust clouds in the Galaxy was compiled by Dutra and Bica (2002) on the basis of 21 previously published catalogues. It contains data on 5004 clouds and complexes of clouds and includes coordinates, apparent dimensions, opacity class, etc. Electronic version of the catalogue can be obtained via anonymous ftp (see Sect. 5.2).

Considerable attention has been given to the construction of the extinction distribution in the areas close to the centre of the Galaxy. These investigations aim at a study of stellar populations and stellar dynamics in the galactic bulge and bar. The extinction maps were obtained in the frame of the DENIS[15] (Schultheis *et al.*, 1999) and 2MASS (Dutra *et al.*, 2003b) surveys and from the gravitational microlensing experiments MACHO (Popowski *et al.*, 2003) and OGLE-II (Sumi, 2003). Besides this, Udalski (2003) inferred that an anomalous extinction existed toward the galactic bulge: the ratio of the total extinction to the selective one R_V was smaller than the average galactic value.

3.2   Interstellar extinction: interpretation

It is now evident that observed interstellar extinction cannot be explain using particles of only one kind. Therefore, three tendencies in the modelling of multi-component dust mixtures are being developed.

---

[15] DENIS — Deep Near Infrared Survey; 2MASS — Two-Micron All-Sky Survey; MACHO — MAssive Compact Halo Objects; OGLE — Optical Gravitational Lensing Experiment.

1. Several populations of compact (usually spherical) grains are used. Populations consist of different materials. The optical properties are calculated from the Mie theory. Such an approach was used many times for the interpretation of the interstellar extinction curves (e.g., Mathis *et al.*, 1977; Zubko *et al.*, 1996) and the SEDs in spectra of stars and YSOs (see Table 8). In the case of circumstellar shells, the authors do not worry about the problem of cosmic abundances and can apply multicomponent mixtures with varying fractional abundances at different distances from an object. For example, Men'shchikov *et al.* (1999) chose a four-component mixture to fit observations of the young star HL Tau. The disadvantage of such an approach is the impossibility of including the vacuum as a component.

2. Several materials are mixed using one of the EMT's rules and then the Mie theory is applied for calculations of the optical properties of such "composite" particles. In this case, there exist many doubts on the validity of employing the EMT for significant fractional abundances of components as is discussed in Sect. 2.1.4.

3. Inhomogeneous (composite) particles with layers or inclusions from different materials or aggregate particles are considered and light scattering computations are made using the DDA, TMM or simpler theory like the Mie theory for n-layered spheres. This approach seems to be the most promising because it allows one to describe more exactly the properties of dust grains. However, calculations with the DDA are very time-consuming and at the present can be used rather for illustrative than for mass calculations (e.g., Wolff *et al.*, 1994; Vaidya *et al.*, 2001). The idea of composite particles as multi-layered spheres (Voshchinnikov and Mathis, 1999; see also Iatì *et al.*, 2001) looks a bit artificial but attractive from the point of view of numerical realization (see discussion in Sect. 3.2.1).

The intensity of radiation at the wavelength λ after passing a dust cloud $I(\lambda)$ is equal to

$$I(\lambda) = I_0(\lambda)\, e^{-\tau(\lambda)}, \qquad (3.29)$$

where $I_0(\lambda)$ is the source (star) intensity and $\tau(\lambda)$ the optical thickness along the line of sight. The interstellar extinction is

$$A(\lambda) = -2.5 \log \frac{I(\lambda)}{I_0(\lambda)} \approx -1.086 \ln e^{-\tau(\lambda)} = 1.086\tau(\lambda). \quad (3.30)$$

Here, $\tau(\lambda)$ is the total extinction cross-section of all type particles along the line of sight in given direction.

For spherical particles of radius r_s, we have

$$A(\lambda) = 1.086 \, \pi r_s^2 \, Q_{ext}(m, r_s, \lambda) \, N_d = 1.086 \, \pi r_s^2 \, Q_{ext}(m, r_s, \lambda) \, n_d \, D, \quad (3.31)$$

where N_d and n_d are the column and number densities of dust grains, correspondingly and D is the distance to the star.

For a polydisperse ensemble, averaging over a size distribution should be performed

$$A(\lambda) = 1.086 \int_{r_{s,-}}^{r_{s,+}} \pi r_s^2 \, Q_{ext}(m, r_s, \lambda) n_d(r_s) \, dr_s \cdot D. \quad (3.32)$$

Here, $n_d(r_s)$ is the size distribution of dust grains with the lower cut-off $r_{s,-}$ and the upper cut-off $r_{s,+}$.

From Eqs. (3.31) and (3.32), the important conclusion follows: *the wavelength dependence of interstellar extinction is totally determined by the wavelength dependence of the extinction efficiencies Q_{ext}.*

3.2.1   Extinction efficiencies: general behaviour and deviations

The extinction efficiency factors Q_{ext} are usually considered as a function of the size parameter $x = 2\pi r/\lambda$ for a fixed refractive index m that, strictly speaking, does not characterize the dependence $Q_{ext}(\lambda)$ because of the wavelength dependence of $m(\lambda)$ (Sect. 2.1.2). The behaviour of $Q_{ext}(x)$ is as follows: initially it rises rapidly with x, has several maxima and minima and goes asymptotically to a constant with a decaying oscillation. This behaviour is typical for weakly absorbing homogeneous spheres (Fig. 18, upper panel; see also Fig. 11). The large-scale oscillations are caused by the interference between

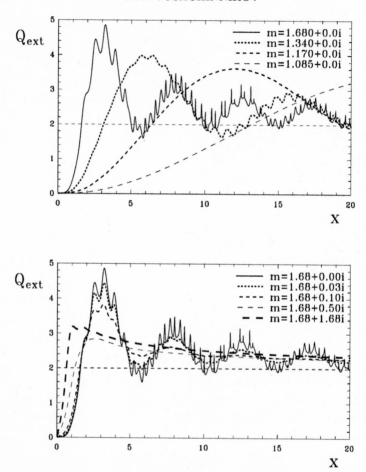

Figure 18 Size dependence of the extinction efficiency factors for homogeneous spherical particles. The influence of variations of the real part (upper panel) and imaginary part (lower panel) of the refractive index is illustrated.

near forward transmission and diffraction (A.R. Jones, 1999). The height of the first peak is always maximal while subsequent peaks become lower and lower. The peak positions are determined by the values of the phase shift $\rho = 2x|m - 1|$ (Sect. 2.2.3; the path of the central ray through the particle). The efficiencies plotted against ρ have maxima at nearly the same positions for different m until the imaginary part of refractive index is small (see, e.g., Martin, 1978).

For large values of x, the extinction factors approach the limiting value 2 (see Eq. (2.73) and Fig. 11). This would suggest that the particle will block off twice the light falling upon it, an effect calling the "extinction paradox" (van de Hulst, 1957; Bohren and Huffman, 1983). Its explanation lies in the fact that two different phenomena are occurring: diffraction and the geometrical optics effects of reflection, refraction and absorption. The efficiency for each of these effects is one and hence

$$Q_{\text{ext}}^{\lim} = Q_{\text{diff}} + Q_{\text{geom}} = 2.$$

If the particle is very large, the diffraction pattern is very narrow. As laboratory detectors (including the human eye) collect light over a finite angular range, the diffracted light is registered and not measured as a loss. The measurement yields

$$Q_{\text{ext}}^{\lim} = Q_{\text{geom}} = 1,$$

as would be expected. However, the conditions in astronomy totally differ from those in the laboratory and the diffracted light is always lost, i.e. *the extinction paradox is present.*

The ripple-like structure in the form of small extremely sharp peaks and troughs is observed for non-absorbing particles if the real part of the refractive index n is large (Figs. 11 and 18). These ripple-like fluctuations result from the resonances of virtual modes (Bohren and Huffman, 1983). From the mathematical point of view, the scattering resonances are associated with zeros of the denominator in the expressions for Mie coefficients. The exclusion of the zeros lies in the basis of the S-approximation discussed in Sect. 2.2.4. Note that the ripples are washed away by any size distribution of particles.

Figure 18 illustrates the effect of variations of the real and imaginary parts of the refractive index and can be used for the prediction of extinction produced by real materials (e.g., given in Table 4). In

particular, it is seen that the largest extinction for a given spherical particle can be obtained for dielectric particles with large values
of n (silicates, quartz, MgO, SiC). At the same time, the extinction
by metals or carbonaceous particles dominates for very small size
parameters (Figs. 12 and 18). The dilution of any material by the
vacuum reduces both n and k (Table 5 and Fig. 5), which causes
a shift and decrease of interference maxima and smoothing of the
extinction curves (Fig. 18).

The behaviour of extinction for spherical particles described above
is considered as typical for extinction factors. The deviations from
it occur when the inhomogeneous or/and non-spherical particles are
examined. Inhomogeneity causes variations of refraction and reflection inside a particle that changes the optical path of the rays. For
non-spherical particles, refraction and reflection on the surfaces with
variable curvature result in alteration of scattering by such particles
in the comparison with that by spheres.

The optical properties of core-mantle spheres were studied rather
well and seems to show no significant peculiarities[16] (Prishivalko *et
al.*, 1984; Babenko *et al.*, 2003). But already three-layered spheres
can produce anomalous extinction of light. This is illustrated in
Fig. 19 where the extinction efficiency factors Q_{ext} are plotted for
spheres consisting of 3, 9 and 15 equivolume layers. The layers are
composed of different materials (amorphous carbon (AC1), astrosil
and vacuum) but the total volume fraction of each constituent is 1/3.
The optical constants for AC1 and astrosil were taken as shown in
Table 4. The peculiar behaviour of extinction is seen on the upper
panel of Fig. 19 for the case of particles with the carbon core and
astrosil as the outermost layer. Here, a very rare situation is observed when the first maximum is damped but there is very broad
second maximum which is the highest. This peculiarity disappears
if the number of layers increases: the difference in curves is hardly
distinguished for particles with 15 layers (lower panel of Fig. 19).
The given fact, noted by Voshchinnikov and Mathis (1999), allows
one to suggest multi-layered particles as a new approximate model of
composite grains. Such a model permits us to include an arbitrary

---

[16] Except for a resonance peak arising for particles with very large refractive
index of a mantle (see, e.g., Gurwich *et al.*, 2003).

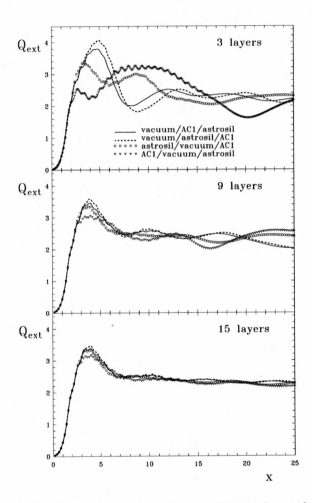

Figure 19 Size dependence of the extinction efficiency factors for multi-layered spherical particles. Each particle contains an equal fraction (33%) of amorphous carbon (AC1), astrosil and vacuum separated in equivolume layers. The cyclic order of the layers is indicated (starting from the core). The effect of the increase of the number of layers is illustrated.

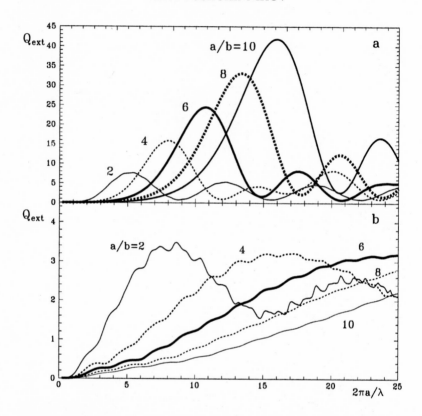

Figure 20 Extinction efficiency factors Q_{ext} at parallel incidence ($\alpha = 0°$) as a function of the size parameter $2\pi a/\lambda$ (a is a major semiaxis of spheroid) for prolate (a) and oblate (b) homogeneous spheroids with the refractive index $m = 1.5 + 0.0i$. The values of the aspect ratio a/b are indicated. After Voshchinnikov (1996).

fraction of any material and its numerical realization requires rather moderate computational resources (see Sect. 3.2.5). The dependence of the extinction efficiency factor Q_{ext} on the parameter $2\pi a/\lambda$ for prolate and oblate spheroids with the refractive index $m = 1.5 + 0.0i$ and the aspect ratio $a/b = 2(2)10$ is shown in Figs. 20 and 21. The normalization used in Fig. 21 gives the possibility of comparing the

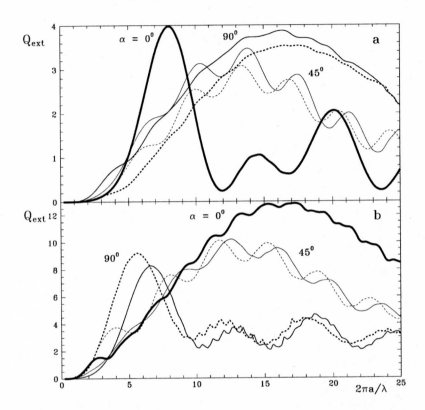

Figure 21 Extinction efficiency factors $Q_{ext} = C_{ext}/(\pi ab)$ as a function of the size parameter $2\pi a/\lambda$ for the prolate (a) and oblate (b) homogeneous spheroids with $m = 1.5 + 0.0i$ and $a/b = 4$. The normalization by πab was made in all cases. The factors for TM (TE) mode are plotted by the solid (dashed) lines. The values of the incident angle α are indicated. After Voshchinnikov (1996).

factors calculated for different orientations of a particle. Large-scale variations of the factor have the same reasons as for spheres. But some features of the behaviour of the factors plotted in Figs. 20a and 21b take place: the third maximum is higher than the second one for prolate spheroids at $\alpha = 0°$ and for oblate spheroids at $\alpha = 90°$ if a/b

= 4 and 6. Asano (1979) found the similar peculiarity for particles with $a/b = 4$ and 5. This phenomenon is determined by the particle shape and orientation and arises for dielectric particles with different ratios a/b (see also Voshchinnikov, 2001).

As seen from Fig. 20a, for prolate spheroids the values of Q_{ext} can be rather large if radiation propagates along the major (rotation) axis of a particle ($\alpha = 0°$). This is a result of normalization by the geometrical cross-section which is small in this case $G(0°) = \pi b^2$ (see Eq. (2.41)). The factors can be even larger for $a/b \gg 1$ (see Fig. 22). As follows from this Figure, the behaviour of the factors for very elongated spheroids is rather regular, and the values of Q_{ext} smoothly decrease with the size parameter. There are 25 maxima on the interval $2\pi a/\lambda = 0$–300, which is totally distinct from the behaviour for spherical particles (cf. Fig. 11). Note that the size of "equivolume" particles x_V considered in Fig. 22 is moderate: from Eq. (2.39) it follows that $x_V \approx 13.92$ if $2\pi a/\lambda = 300$ and $a/b = 100$. But the path of light inside a spheroidal particle is in $300/13.92 \approx 21.5$ times longer than inside a sphere of the same volume.

It is significant that the limiting value of the extinction factors for particles of any shape must be equal to 2 but as is seen from the inset in Fig. 22 this condition is far for being satisfied although the tendency to reduction of Q_{ext} is observed.

Figures 20 and 21 also show that ripple-like fluctuations are better seen for the oblate spheroids than for the prolate ones. The ripples vanish from sight for elongated (prolate) spheroids if α approaches zero. A similar picture is observed for infinite cylinders (Fig. 23). In this Figure, the extinction efficiencies for prolate spheroids and infinitely long circular cylinders are compared.

The simplest model of non-spherical particles — infinite circular cylinders — is not physically reasonable. However, it looks attractive to find cases when this model could be useful because calculations in this case are very simple and fast. Previous attempts to find the limits of applicability of the model of infinite cylinders were made by Martin (1978) and Voshchinnikov (1990). In both cases, particles of the same thickness were considered, i.e. spheroids and cylinders had the equal size parameters $2\pi a_{\text{cyl}}/\lambda = 2\pi b/\lambda$. Martin (1978) notes that the factors for spheroids resemble those for cylinders if $a/b \gtrsim 4$ for the normal incidence of radiation ($\alpha = 90°$) but in order to align

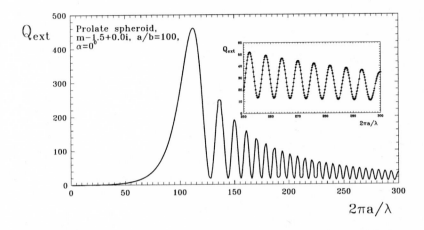

Figure 22 Extinction efficiency factors for elongated spheroidal particles in dependence on the size parameter $2\pi a/\lambda$. After Voshchinnikov and Farafonov (2002).

the peaks in extinction, the x-scale for cylinders was stretched by a factor 1.13.

Voshchinnikov and Farafonov (2002) established a similarity of the behaviour of the efficiency factors: both TM and TE-modes for spheroids converge to some limiting values which are close to those of infinite cylinders. This occurs if the size parameter is defined in a special way — both the volume and the aspect ratio of a spheroid and a very long cylinder with the length $2L$ are put to be the same, i.e. $V_{\text{spheroid}} = V_{\text{cyl}}$ and $a/b = L/a_{\text{cyl}}$. So, we need to compare the particles with size parameters $2\pi a_{\text{cyl}}/\lambda$ and $2\pi b/\lambda \cdot (2/3)^{1/3}$ as it is shown in Fig. 23. Note that the scaling factor $[(3/2)^{1/3} \approx 1.145]$ which arises is close to that empirically found by Martin (1978). For the normal and oblique incidence of radiation ($30° \lesssim \alpha \leq 90°$), the efficiency factors converge to some limit values with an increase of the aspect ratio a/b, provided spheroids of the same volume and thickness are considered. These values are close to, but do not coincide with the factors for infinite cylinders (see Voshchinnikov and Farafonov, 2002 for more details).

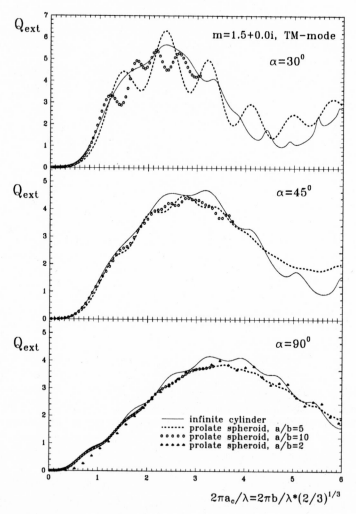

Figure 23 Extinction efficiency factors (TM mode) for prolate spheroids ($Q_{ext} = C_{ext}/G(\alpha)$) and infinite cylinders ($Q_{ext} = C_{ext}/(2a_{cyl}\sin\alpha)$) as a function of the size parameter $2\pi a_{cyl}/\lambda = 2\pi b/\lambda \cdot (2/3)^{1/3}$. After Voshchinnikov and Farafonov (2002).

3.2.2   Wavelength dependence

Interpretation of the interstellar extinction involves two tasks: explanation of the wavelength dependence and fitting the absolute extinction. The first task assumes the searching for chemical composition and sizes of particles which give the wavelength dependence of the extinction efficiencies close to the observed dependence of $A^{(n)}(\lambda)$. The average interstellar extinction curve in the visible-near UV ($1\,\mu m \leq \lambda^{-1} \leq 3\,\mu m$) presented in Fig. 13 can be approximated by the power law $A(\lambda) \propto \lambda^{-1.33}$. This dependence is plotted in Figs. 24–26 as a dashed segment. The Figures allow one to judge the influence of the size, chemical composition, structure and shape of particles on the wavelength dependence of extinction. In all cases, the initial growth of extinction reflects the increase of factors $Q_{ext}(m, x)$ at the interval from zero up to the first maximum. As follows from Fig. 24, spheres of astrosil with $r_s \approx 0.1\,\mu m$ or slightly smaller spheres of AC1 can produce the dependence $A(\lambda)$ resembling the observed one. Evidently, the fraction of particles with these radii in the size distribution must be considerable. As was noted many times (e.g., Greenberg, 1978), a similar extinction occurs if the product of the typical particle size $\langle r \rangle$ on the particle refractive index is constant, i.e.

$$\langle r \rangle |m - 1| \approx \text{const.} \qquad (3.33)$$

Using the values of m from Table 4 and the results shown in Fig. 24, it is possible to conclude that the wavelength dependence of extinction in the visible can be approximately reproduced if one choose the particles of astrosil with $r_s \approx 0.1\,\mu m$, particles of AC1 with $r_s \approx 0.08\,\mu m$, particles of iron with $r_s \approx 0.04\,\mu m$, etc. This illustrates that *from the wavelength dependence of extinction one can determine only the product of the typical particle size on refractive index but not the size or chemical composition of dust grains separately.*

The conclusion on the impossibility to identify exactly the structure of particles can be done from Fig. 25 where the extinction for spheres with a fraction of vacuum is presented. The voids were included in two ways: using the Bruggeman mixing rule (see Table 5) and in the form of the core in core-mantle spheres. In both cases, the "effective" refractive index of particles reduces, and according

N.V. VOSHCHINNIKOV

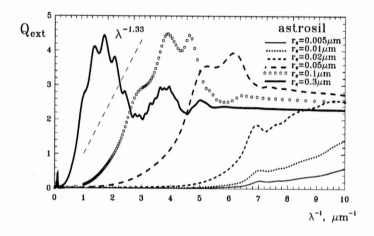

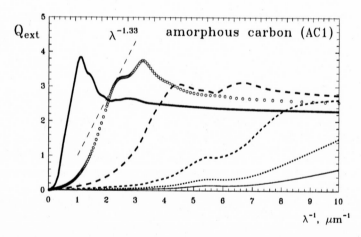

Figure 24 Wavelength dependence of the extinction efficiency factors for homogeneous spherical particles of different sizes consisting of astronomical silicate and amorphous carbon. The dashed segment shows the approximate wavelength dependence of the mean galactic extinction curve at optical wavelengths.

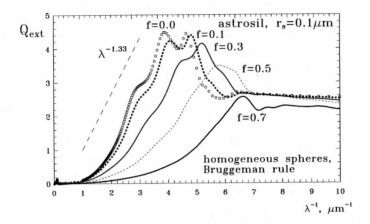

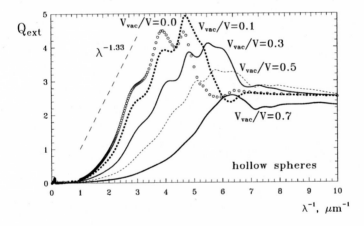

Figure 25 Wavelength dependence of the extinction efficiency factors for spherical particles of astronomical silicate with radius $r_s = 0.1\,\mu m$. Calculations were made for homogeneous particles with the refractive indices found from the Bruggeman mixing rule with a different fraction of vacuum (upper panel) and for hollow particles with different core size (lower panel). The dashed segment shows the approximate wavelength dependence of the mean galactic extinction curve at optical wavelengths.

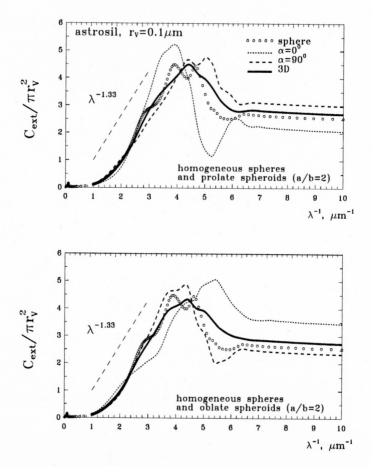

Figure 26 Wavelength dependence of the normalized extinction cross-sections for spherical and spheroidal equivolume particles of astronomical silicate with radius $r_V = 0.1\,\mu$m. Calculations were made for homogeneous spheroids with $a/b = 2$ in a fixed orientation ($\alpha = 0°$ and $90°$) and for 3D-orientation. The dashed segment shows the approximate wavelength dependence of the mean galactic extinction curve at optical wavelengths.

to Eq. (3.33) to produce the observed extinction, the particle radius over $r_s = 0.1\,\mu m$ must be increased. It is interesting to note the similarity in behaviour of extinction for particles with different internal structure. This shows that the EMT is not a totally hopeless matter.

In Fig. 26, the normalized extinction cross-sections $C_{ext}/\pi r_V^2$ for spheroids (see Eqs. (2.43) and (2.44)) and spheres are plotted. The results for spheroids are shown for two orientations of non-rotating particles ("picket fence" alignment) and for the case of the arbitrary orientation in space (3D alignment) when the average cross-section is:

$$\langle C_{ext}\rangle^{3D} = \int_0^{\pi/2} \frac{1}{2}\left[Q_{ext}^{TM}(\alpha) + Q_{ext}^{TE}(\alpha)\right] G(\alpha)\,\sin\alpha\,d\alpha. \qquad (3.34)$$

Here G is the geometrical cross-section of a spheroid (Eqs. (2.41) and (2.42)) and the incident radiation is assumed to be non-polarized. Figure 26 shows that the shape of particles has a small influence on the extinction at different wavelengths. Certainly, the curves for spheroids in a fixed orientation differ from those for spheres, and the difference increases with the growth of a/b. However, the wavelength dependence of extinction close to the observed one can be obtained if the difference in the paths of the rays inside particles with different orientation is taken into account. It means that the particles with r_V smaller than 0.1 μm for $\alpha = 0°$ (90°) and larger than 0.1 μm for $\alpha = 90°$ (0°) for prolate (oblate) particles should be chosen.

Thus, neither chemical composition, nor structure, and shape of dust particles can be uniquely deduced from the wavelength dependence of the interstellar extinction.

Note also that the extinction in the visible part of spectrum becomes wavelength-independent (neutral) if the particle radius exceeds several microns as it follows from Fig. 27.

3.2.3   The λ 2175 Å feature

Laboratory and theoretical modelling of the UV bump on the interstellar extinction curve is a very popular topic in dusty investigations. Since the discovery of the bump by Stecher (1965) and its first explanations (Wickramasinghe and Guillaume, 1965; Stecher and Donn,

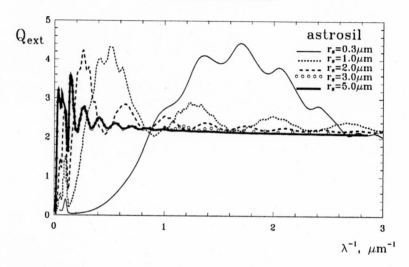

Figure 27 Extinction efficiency factors for homogeneous spherical particles of different sizes consisting of astronomical silicate. If $r_s \geq 2 - 3\,\mu m$, the wavelength dependence of Q_{ext} is barely perceptible at optical wavelengths.

1965), consideration proceeded in the following directions: search for carrier candidates, improvement of the optical constants (mainly for graphite being the most likely candidate) and application of more progressive light scattering theories which give the possibility of including the particle shape and material anisotropy effects. Among possible candidates, silicate (enstatite), irradiated quartz, oxides (MgO, CaO), organic molecules were considered too. However, carbonaceous species and especially graphite are the favourite material. The number of different explanations of the UV bump (both successful and failed) using carbon-based materials is rather large. They include consideration of both ordered and disordered forms of carbon: graphite, amorphous and graphitic carbons, coals, quenched carbonaceous composites, PAHs, carbonaceous (amorphous/glassy) particles (see Mennella *et al.*, 1998 and references therein). The use of well-ordered carbon like graphite is preferable because of smaller amount of carbon required although perfectly ordered, true graphite is unlikely to be present in the interstellar medium[17]. Experiments also show that the UV bump can be matched up with absorption features from high purity, well-dispersed annealed carbon onions (Chhowalla *et al.*, 2003).

The problem is to interpret simultaneously the central position of the peak and its width[18]. Unfortunately, this problem does not have unique solution: the observations can be explained, for example, by the effects of coating (Mathis, 1994), clumping (Rouleau *et al.*, 1997) or clustering (Schnaiter *et al.*, 1998) of the isolated carbon particles.

The contradictoriness of identification of the λ 2175 Å feature is illustrated by Fig. 28 where the profiles were calculated using the model of graphite spheres. The anisotropic dielectric functions for graphite were taken from Laor and Draine (1993) and so-called "2/3–1/3" approximation for the averaged extinction factors was employed

$$Q_{\text{ext}} = \frac{2}{3} Q_{\text{ext}}(\varepsilon_\perp) + \frac{1}{3} Q_{\text{ext}}(\varepsilon_{||}), \qquad (3.35)$$

where $\varepsilon_\perp$ and $\varepsilon_{||}$ are the dielectric functions for two cases of orientation of the electric field relative to the basal plane of graphite and the efficiencies $Q_{\text{ext}}(\varepsilon_\perp)$ and $Q_{\text{ext}}(\varepsilon_{||})$ are calculated with the Mie theory. Using the DDA, Draine and Malhotra (1994) showed that the "2/3–1/3" approximation was sufficiently accurate in studying the extinction profile of the λ 2175 Å feature: in the range $\lambda^{-1} = 3.5$–$5.0\,\mu\text{m}^{-1}$ the maximum error was approximately $6(r_s/0.04\,\mu\text{m})\%$, for $r_s \lesssim 0.04\,\mu\text{m}$.

As follows from Fig. 28, the profiles with the central position near $\lambda_0^{-1} = 4.6\,\mu\text{m}^{-1}$ can be obtained if we take the compact spheres with radius $r_s = 0.015\,\mu\text{m}$ (upper panel) or hollow spheres with $r_s = 0.010\,\mu\text{m}$ and $V_{\text{vac}}/V = 0.1$ (middle panel). Although for single-size particles the width of the calculated profiles is smaller than the observed one, a simple bi-modal size distribution allows one to fit both the position and the width of the mean galactic profile (Fig. 28, lower panel).

---

[17] Crystalline graphite has a strong resonant feature near λ 11.52 μm (Draine, 1984) which is not observed.

[18] Note that the observed weakness of the bump strength in dense clouds can be attributed to the hydrogenation of carbon (Sorrell, 1990).

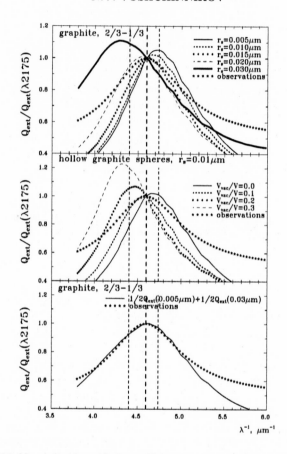

Figure 28 Normalized extinction efficiencies for graphite spheres. The calculations were made for homogeneous particles (upper panel) and hollow particles with a different fraction of vacuum (middle panel). The curve marked as "observations" corresponds to the wavelength dependence of the UV bump given by the mean galactic extinction curve (Sect. 3.1.2). The central position of the observed UV bump and its range of variations are marked. The lower panel shows the summary extinction of two graphite spheres with radii $r_s = 0.005\,\mu m$ and $r_s = 0.03\,\mu m$ (from upper panel) taken in equal proportions. All calculations were made in the "2/3–1/3" approximation (Eq. (3.35)).

Note that the shape effects cannot be identified from extinction measurements (see, e.g., Draine and Malhotra, 1994; Mathis, 1994). Duley and Seahra (1998) investigated extinction produced by small carbon particles consisting of aromatic rings in configurations similar to those of PAH molecules. They found that the changes of the bump position and width could be attributed to the variations of the degrees of hydrogenation, ionization and defects.

So, we can conclude that *identification of the λ 2175 Å feature is still a problem without a single solution, especially if only the extinction profile is considered.*

3.2.4   Absolute extinction and abundances

Along with the wavelength dependence, it is important to reproduce the *absolute value of extinction* using the dust-phase abundances found for a given direction $[X/H]_d$ (Sect. 2.1.1). These abundances can be expressed via

- observed quantities: interstellar extinction A_V and hydrogen column density $N(H)$;

- model parameters: mass of constituents in a grain m_i, the relative part of the element X in the constituent i, n_i^X, density of grain material ρ_i and relative volume of the constituent in a particle V_i/V and

- a calculated quantity: the ratio of the extinction cross-section to the particle volume C_{ext}/V.

Assuming that the spherical dust grains are inhomogeneous (i.e., composed of several species) and have the same radius r_s we obtain from Eq. (3.31) that

$$\left[\frac{X}{H}\right]_d = \frac{A_V}{1.086N(H)} \left[\frac{C_{ext}(\lambda_V)}{V}\right]^{-1} \sum_i \frac{\rho_i}{m_i} n_i^X \frac{V_i}{V}$$

$$= 1.228 \cdot 10^6 \, R_V \left[\frac{N(H)}{E(B-V)}\right]^{-1} \frac{r_s}{Q_{ext}(\lambda_V)} \sum_i \frac{\rho_i}{m_i} n_i^X \frac{V_i}{V}. \quad (3.36)$$

Here, the summation is performed over all constituents of a given kind of grains, abundances are in ppm. To minimize the value of $[X/H]_d$ (to save the material), the ratio C_{ext}/V (or Q_{ext}/r_s) should be taken as large as possible, which occurs near the first maximum on the extinction curves. As follows from Fig. 18, the maximum extinction takes place when the real part of the refractive index is large while the imaginary part is small. According to Table 4, this is typical of dielectric particles like silicates or SiC.

In order to explain the absolute extinction of the star ζ Oph (HD 149757; $A_V = 0^m94^{(19)}$), using homogeneous spherical particles, the minimum abundance of carbon must be 320 ppm in the case of amorphous carbon (AC1) and 267 ppm in the case of graphite (the dust-phase value is 110 ppm, see Table 3). If the particles are of astrosil ($MgFeSiO_4$), 52.5 ppm of Fe, Mg and Si and 211 ppm of O are required. All these abundances are also larger than the observed dust-phase ones[20].

Mixing several materials in one particle, we can reduce the demand. Estimates of the dust-phase abundances of the five main elements are plotted in Fig. 29 for the case of multi-layered spheres already discussed in Sect. 3.2.1. The particles consisting of AC1, astrosil and vacuum are considered. The volume fraction of one constituent (AC1 or astrosil) was fixed while that of another constituent varied. The rest of the particle volume is assumed to be occupied by a vacuum. Because of the complicated behaviour of extinction, the relation between the model parameter V_i/V and the dust-phase abundance $[X/H]_d$ given by Eq. (3.36) is non-linear. As a result, two families of curves are obtained as is clearly seen in Fig. 29. One family is related to the particles with small volume fraction of astrosil ($V_{asil}/V = 0.1$) and increasing volume fraction of carbon. Three curves of this family are the lowest ones in the middle and lower panels of Fig. 29, i.e. growing the amount of carbon in grains we reduce the requirements on the dust-phase abundances of magnesium, sili-

---

[19] This value is obtained from Eq. (3.19) and colour excess $E(V - K) = 0^m84$ (Serkowski *et al.*, 1975). According to Skórzyński *et al.* (2003), the neutral extinction in the direction of this star seems to be absent: $A_0 = 0^m10^{+0.58}_{-0.60}$.

[20] The densities of materials $\rho = 1.85$ g/cm^3 for AC1, $\rho = 2.25$ g/cm^3 for graphite and $\rho = 3.3$ g/cm^3 for astrosil were taken.

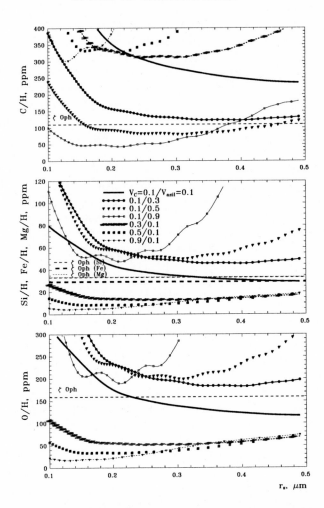

Figure 29 The dust-phase abundances of the five main elements required for the explanation of the visual extinction for the star ζ Oph using multi-layered spheres. The particles consist of some amount of AC1 and astrosil as indicated. The rest of the volume is occupied by a vacuum. The dust-phase abundances in the direction of ζ Oph (see Table 3) are shown by horizontal lines.

con, iron and oxygen. But at the same time, the curves from this family hold the uppermost positions in the upper panel of Fig. 29 resulting in very large abundance of carbon in comparison with the observed one. Figure 29 shows that no variations of the volume fractions can simultaneously satisfy to the required dust-phase abundances for all five elements. The most strict demands are connected with the abundances of C and Fe but they can be slightly reduced as one can replace one of the constituents (silicate or carbon) by iron carbide (FeC).

It is also interesting to consider whether changing the grain shape can enlarge the ratio C_{ext}/V. Mathis (1996) analyzed the shape effects for spheroidal particles using the Rayleigh and geometrical optics approximations and results of the calculations of Asano and Sato (1980). He concluded that the extinction cross-sections for spheroids are larger than those of spheres of same volume and increased all values of C_{ext} calculated for spheres by a factor 1.09.

In reality, as Fig. 30 shows the extinction by prolate and oblate equivolume spheroids can be larger or smaller than that of spheres depending on the particle shape, size and orientation. From Fig. 30 it follows that for silicate particles variations of the ratio C_{ext}(spheroid)$/C_{ext}$(sphere) are from ~ 0.7 to ~ 1.4 if the particle aspect ratio $a/b = 2$. These limits shift to ~ 0.4 to ~ 2.2 for $a/b = 5$[21]. Although spheroids in a fixed orientation can give a rise of extinction at some sizes, the extinction by non-aligned particles (3D orientation) turns around the extinction by spheres (Fig. 30). As interstellar grains are aligned, slightly enhanced extinction can arise for large particles as demonstrated by the curve for $\alpha = 90°$ plotted in the lower panel of Fig. 30. Since the interstellar particles rotate around their small axes, this curve also corresponds to the perfectly aligned rotating grains when the direction of orientation (magnetic field) is perpendicular to the line of sight (see discussion in Part II, Sect. 8).

Finally, we can note that it seems improbable that there exists a still unknown material or light scattering theory allowing one to increase significantly the value of extinction although a chance for some enhancement with known materials and multi-layered non-spherical

---

[21] In a similar manner, extinction varies for particles of another chemical composition.

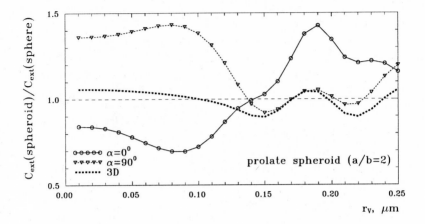

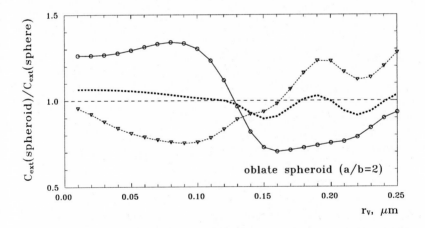

Figure 30 The ratio of the extinction cross-sections C_{ext} for prolate and oblate spheroids and spheres of the same volume. The particles are of astronomical silicate (refractive index of Table 4). Calculations were made for homogeneous spheroids with $a/b = 2$ at fixed orientations ($\alpha = 0°$ and $90°$) and with 3D-orientation.

particles still remains. We cannot expect either large errors or wrong results in the determination of the gas-phase abundances. Therefore, the only possible way to resolve the problem is a thorough analysis of cosmic abundances. Very probably, they are not the same in different galactic regions. Another possibility to solve the dilemma would be to argue that stars do not, in fact, represent the composition of the interstellar gas plus dust. This heretical idea is discussed by Snow (2000) who suggests that the mysteries should be resolved with the aid of the new instruments FUSE (Far Ultraviolet Spectroscopic Explorer) and Chandra. These cosmic observatories are able to observe faint objects and provide information on the total interstellar composition (gas plus dust, through the X-ray absorption edges, Chandra) as well as strongly extend our knowledge of hydrogen abundances, depletions and far-UV extinction (FUSE). On the basis of the observations made to date new information could be inferred only by the cosmic abundance of oxygen in several directions. Using the Chandra high resolution spectrum of the object Cyg X-2, Takei $et\ al.$ (2002) estimated the dust-phase (179 ppm) and total (579 ppm) abundances of oxygen. The latter is larger than the solar one presented in Table 3 (490 ppm). However, Juett $et\ al.$ (2003) found the value of $[O/H]_{cosmic} \approx 478$ ppm for the same object. They investigated the oxygen K-shell interstellar absorption edge in seven X-ray binaries and evaluated the total O abundances. These abundances lie in the limits from 467 ppm to 492 ppm, which is in a good agreement with the solar abundance in the new reference system. Relying on the observations from HST and FUSE André $et\ al.$ (2003) measured the interstellar gas-phase oxygen abundances along the sight lines toward 19 early-type stars at distances from 840 pc to 5010 pc. A mean abundance is $[O/H]_g = 408$ ppm (extreme values are 309 ppm and 512 ppm) which gives for a mean dust-phase abundance $[O/H]_d = 82$ ppm. However, the mean of Meyer $et\ al.$ (1998) sample of 13 stars at distances smaller than 1 kpc is $[O/H]_g = 319$ ppm. This fact strongly suggests that the regional variations of abundances is a reality. Note also that Schulz $et\ al.$ (2002) evaluated the total abundance of iron towards the object Cyg X-1 $[O/H]_{cosmic} \approx 25$ ppm.

3.2.5   Some steps in the modelling of extinction

Since the first works on the interpretation of the interstellar extinction and till now, the main goal of the modellers was to reconstruct the dust size distribution using the particles of some chemical composition related with the cosmic abundances. For the first time, the grain size distribution was found in tabular form by Oort and van de Hulst (1946). Later, Greenberg (1968) fitted it by the exponential equation

$$n(r_s) \propto \exp\left[-5\left(\frac{r_s}{r_{s0}}\right)^3\right], \qquad (3.37)$$

where r_{s0} is the parameter related to the mean size of grains. The index of degree in Eq. (3.37) was obtained from a physical idea: Greenberg (1968) suggested that the spherical particles grew by accretion and destructed in grain-grain collisions. The probability of the latter process is proportional to πr_s^2 which results in the index "3" in Eq. (3.37). However, as was shown by Isobe (1973), the extinction curves can be fitted using size distributions with different indices if the value of r_{s0} is scaled.

For core-mantle particles, Hong and Greenberg (1980) modified the expression Eq. (3.37) assuming that all particles had the same core radius $r_{s,core}$ and the exponential distribution of mantle radii

$$n(r_s) \propto \exp\left[-5\left(\frac{r_s - r_{s,core}}{r_{s0}}\right)^3\right]. \qquad (3.38)$$

A distribution of this type suggests that all particles formed in stellar atmospheres have the same radius and are covered with mantles of different thickness in interstellar clouds.

Using minimization of the χ^2 statistic, Mathis et al. (1977) reconstructed the power-law size distribution for silicate and graphite particles in the form

$$n(r_s) \propto r_s^{-3.5}. \qquad (3.39)$$

This MRN mixture was used many times in radiative transfer modelling (see Table 8).

The methods developed previously to solve inverse problems were also applied to finding the size distributions from extinction measurements. Kim *et al.* (1994) implemented the maximum entropy method (MEM) to extract a power-law size distribution with exponential decay above some critical size r_{sb}

$$n(r_s) \propto r_s^{-\gamma} \exp(-r_s/r_{sb}). \tag{3.40}$$

Mathis (1996) complicated Eq. (3.40)

$$n(r_s) \propto r_s^{-\gamma_0} \exp[-(\gamma_1 r_s + \gamma_2/r_s + \gamma_3/r_s^2)]. \tag{3.41}$$

Its functional form somewhat resembles a power law (through γ_0) with exponential cut-offs at large (via γ_1 and γ_3) and small (via γ_2) sizes. Note that the size distributions given by Eqs. (3.37)–(3.41) can be used for non-spherical particles as well. For example, Hong and Greenberg (1980) considered infinite cylinders in such a way. In this case, r_s is replaced by r_{cyl}, the radius of a cylindrical particle.

Weingartner and Draine (2001) constructed the size distributions for carbonaceous (C) and silicate (Si) grains taking into account very small carbonaceous particles (PAHs). Its functional form allows one to get a smooth cut-off for radii $r_s > r_{st}$ with control of the steepness of this cut-off and to change the slope of size distribution for $r_s < r_{st}$. The following form was suggested:

$$n(r_s) \propto \mathcal{D}_C(r_s) + \frac{\mathcal{C}_{C,Si}}{r_s} \left(\frac{r_s}{r_{st;C,Si}} \right)^{\alpha_{C,Si}}$$

$$\times \left\{ \begin{array}{ll} 1 + \beta_{C,Si} r_s/r_{st;C,Si}, & \beta \geq 0 \\ (1 - \beta_{C,Si} r_s/r_{st;C,Si})^{-1}, & \beta < 0 \end{array} \right\} \tag{3.42}$$

$$\times \left\{ \begin{array}{ll} 1 & 3.5\,\text{Å} < r_s < r_{st;C,Si} \\ \exp\{-[(r_s - r_{st;C,Si})/r_{st;C,Si}]^3\}, & r_s > r_{st;C,Si}. \end{array} \right.$$

Here, the term $\mathcal{D}_C(r_s)$ is the sum of two log-normal size distributions for very small hydrocarbon molecules which reproduce the diffuse galactic IR emission (see Li and Draine, 2001). The size distribution in the form (3.42) contains 11 parameters (six for carbon and five for silicate).

Zubko *et al.* (1996, 1998) applied Tikhonov's method of regularization, which did not need any preliminary information on the dust grain size distribution. The obtained size distributions can be multi-modal and differ for each component of dust mixture. They have a smooth decay at small sizes and a sharp decay at large sizes. The peaks in size distributions lie near the grain size where the ratio C_{ext}/V is maximal. The same method was used by Zubko *et al.* (2003) in order to fit simultaneously the interstellar extinction and the diffuse IR radiation. After an analysis of a series of models containing PAHs, bare and composite particles Zubko *et al.* (2003) arrived to the conclusion about the ambiguity of models.

Note that in major cases one considered only the average galactic extinction curve which may strongly differ in the UV from the extinction in the direction of individual stars (see Fig. 14). The UV extinction out to 925 Å for three stars was studied by Aannestad (1995). Li and Greenberg (1998) and Larson *et al.* (2000) investigated extinction and polarization in the direction of the star HD 210121. In the modelling of extinction, Li and Greenberg (1998) used ISM cosmic abundances from Snow and Witt (1996), while Larson *et al.* (2000) were oriented towards solar abundances (see Table 3). However, both models require more carbon and silicon than is available in the dust-phase. One more attempt to model extinction for HD 210121 was undertaken by Weingartner and Draine (2001) who applied the size distribution given by Eq. (3.42). Although the required abundance of carbon was found in the bounds given by the old solar abundances, the dust-phase abundance of silicon is ∼ 1.4 times larger than the solar one. The MEM algorithm was employed by Clayton *et al.* (2003b) for fitting the interstellar extinction curves in the wavelength range $0.125–3\,\mu m$ for 7 stars. In order to explain the observations the dust-phase abundances of carbon and silicon must fall in the range 131–198 ppm for C and 36–49 ppm for Si. Requirements on abundances may be reduced if one considers the composite particles.

An important step in understanding of the interstellar extinction was made by Zubko *et al.* (1996, 1998) who considered extinction toward three stars located apparently behind a single interstellar cloud. However, the attempt to satisfy the dust-phase abundances found by Snow and Witt (1996) for ζ Oph failed.

A self-consistent model of extinction in the direction of ζ Oph was constructed by Dubkova (2001; see also Voshchinnikov *et al.*, 2003). She considered extinction by multi-layered porous and com-

N.V. VOSHCHINNIKOV

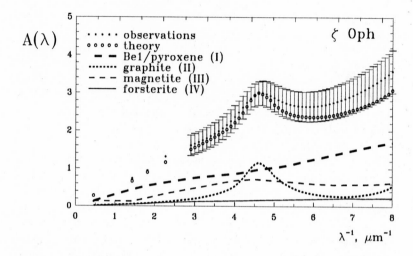

Figure 31 Observed and calculated extinction in the direction of the star ζ Oph. Bold dashed lines show the errors of the parameterization of the observed curve as given by Fitzpatrick and Massa (1990). The contribution to the calculated extinction from different components is shown. After Voshchinnikov *et al.* (2003).

pact spheres with different size distributions. The results are shown in Fig. 31. The model includes four components.

- (I). Porous composite (multi-layered) grains (amorphous carbon, Be1 — 5%; pyroxene, $Fe_{0.5}Mg_{0.5}SiO_3$ — 5%; vacuum — 90%) with the power-law size distribution having an exponential decay.

- (II). Small compact graphite grains with a narrow power-law size distribution.

- (III). Porous composite grains of magnetite (Fe_3O_4 — 2%; vacuum — 98%) with a power-law size distribution.

- (IV). Compact grains of forsterite (Mg_2SiO_4) with a power-law size distribution.

The calculated dust-phase abundances in the direction of ζ Oph are 195 ppm for C, 128 ppm for O, 25 ppm for Mg, 30 ppm for Si and 34 ppm for Si. The observed dust-phase abundances (cf. Table. 3) are lower than the calculated ones for C and Fe. Note that used dust-phase abundances in the direction of ζ Oph are related to the new reference system deduced by Lodders (2003) and, possibly, do not correspond to the regional abundances. However, an attempt to find early-type stars with measured abundances of dust-forming elements in the region around ζ Oph was unsuccessful (Dubkova, 2001).

Summarizing the discussion of interstellar extinction, it is possible to conclude that *any particles do for explanation of the wavelength dependence of extinction and no particles produce the absolute extinction in new reference system of cosmic abundances.*

3.3 Interstellar polarization: observations

3.3.1 Linear polarization and Serkowski's curve

The phenomenon of interstellar linear polarization is related to the effect of the *linear dichroism* of the ISM which results from the presence of aligned non-spherical grains. Such particles produce different extinction of light depending on the orientation of the electric vector of incident radiation relative to the particle axis. The linear polarization is characterized by the polarization degree P and the positional angle θ_E or θ_G measured in the equatorial or galactic coordinates, respectively. Historically, the direction of starlight polarization is associated with the orientation of the plane-of-the-sky component of interstellar magnetic field, $B_\perp$. The data of polarimetric surveys together with other observations like Zeeman splitting of the H I line are used for the study of the magnetic field structure at different scales (see, e.g., Heiles, 1996, 1997). Usually, the pattern of stellar polarization vectors for an interstellar cloud has a rather complicated structure. There are also regional variations of polarization (see discussion in Whittet, 1992 and Sect. 3.3.3).

Many efforts are put into studies of the *wavelength dependence* of polarization. Now it is known in the spectral range $\lambda\,0.12\text{--}12\,\mu$m (Whittet, 1996a). The polarization degree usually has a maximum

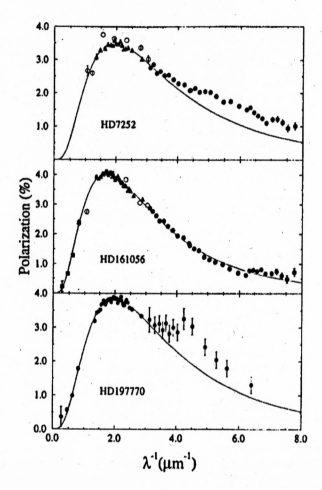

Figure 32 Polarization curves for three stars with different behaviour of the UV polarization. Solid curves fit the visible and near IR data using only Serkowski's curve (Eq. (3.43)) and the relation given by Eq. (3.46). After Whittet (1996a).

in visible and declines in the IR and UV (Fig. 32). The positional angle is weakly wavelength-dependent. Sometimes, its variations reach several degrees and can be explained by changing the alignment direction of dust grains in the line of sight (Martin, 1974).

Serkowski (1973) suggested an empirical formula for the description of the dependence $P(\lambda)$ in the visible part of spectrum

$$P(\lambda)/P_{\max} = \exp[-K \ln^2(\lambda_{\max}/\lambda)]. \qquad (3.43)$$

Initially, the *Serkowski's curve* or *relation* had only two parameters: the maximum degree of polarization $P_{\max}$ and the wavelength corresponding to it $\lambda_{\max}$. The coefficient K was chosen by Serkowski (1973) to be equal to 1.15.

The values of $P_{\max}$ in the diffuse ISM commonly do not exceed 10%. The ratio $P_{\max}/E(B-V)$ determines the *polarizing efficiency* of the interstellar medium in selected direction. There exists an empirically found upper limit on this ratio (Serkowski *et al.*, 1975)

$$P_{\max}/E(B-V) \lesssim 9\%/\text{mag}. \qquad (3.44)$$

The mean value of $\lambda_{\max}$ is $0.55\,\mu$m although there are directions for which $\lambda_{\max}$ is smaller than $0.4\,\mu$m (Whittet *et al.*, 1992; Whittet, 2003) or, possibly, larger than $1\,\mu$m (Goodman *et al.*, 1995). Whittet and van Breda (1978) established a relation between parameters of the extinction and polarization curves

$$R_V = (5.6 \pm 0.3)\,\lambda_{\max},$$

where $\lambda_{\max}$ is in μm. The correlation between extinction and polarization indicates that the same particles are responsible for both phenomena.

The coefficient K characterizes the width of the normalized curve of interstellar linear polarization $W = \lambda_{\max}(\lambda_-^{-1} - \lambda_+^{-1})$, where $\lambda_- < \lambda_{\max} < \lambda_+$ and $P(\lambda_+)/P_{\max} = P(\lambda_-)/P_{\max} = 1/2$. The connection between W and K is given by the relation

$$W = \exp[(\ln 2/K)^{1/2}] - \exp[-(\ln 2/K)^{1/2}]. \qquad (3.45)$$

Using data on IR polarization of 30 stars and treating K as a third free parameter, Wilking *et al.* (1982) deduced the dependence

$$K = (1.86 \pm 0.09)\lambda_{\max} + (-0.10 \pm 0.05). \qquad (3.46)$$

Whittet *et al.* (1992) evaluated this dependence on the basis of observations for 109 stars

$$K = (1.66 \pm 0.09)\lambda_{\max} + (0.01 \pm 0.05). \qquad (3.47)$$

The linear function (3.47) describes the correlation between K and $\lambda_{\max}$ in the Taurus dark cloud quite well but shows strong deviations from it for the ρ Oph cloud (Whittet *et al.*, 1992).

The IR continuum polarization for $\lambda > 2.5\,\mu$m cannot be represented by Serkowski's curve with three parameters. As was noted by Martin and Whittet (1990) and Martin *et al.* (1992), interstellar polarization in the IR seems to have a common, universal functional form independent of the value of $\lambda_{\max}$. Its wavelength dependence is given by a power law

$$P(\lambda) \propto \lambda^{-\hat{\beta}}$$

with $\hat{\beta}$ typically in the range 1.6–2.0.

Interstellar UV polarization was measured on HST and during the Wisconsin Ultraviolet Photo-Polarimeter Experiment (WUPPE)[22]. The final data set was analyzed by Martin *et al.* (1999). It includes 28 lines of sight in the Galaxy. The UV polarization was fitted by a Serkowski'-like curve with the coefficient

$$K_{\mathrm{UV}} = (2.56 \pm 0.38)\lambda_{\max} + (-0.59 \pm 0.21). \qquad (3.48)$$

Three examples of the behaviour of polarization are shown in Fig. 32. The solid curves fit the ground-based data using only Serkowski's curve (Eq. (3.43)) and the relation between K and $\lambda_{\max}$ given by Eq. (3.46). In the case of HD 161056 ($\lambda_{\max} = 0.59\,\mu$m, Fig. 32, middle panel), UV polarization agrees well with the extrapolated curve ("Serkowski's behaviour"). HD 7252 ($\lambda_{\max} = 0.52\,\mu$m) displays a clear excess over the extrapolated curve ("super-Serkowski's behaviour"). HD 197770 ($\lambda_{\max} = 0.51\,\mu$m) shows tentative evidence for polarization excess associated with the extinction bump near λ 2175 Å. Note that only in two directions definitive polarization features have been discovered although the bump is a common attribute of all extinction curves (Martin *et al.*, 1999).

---

[22] Observational data are available via Internet, see the address in Sect. 5.2.

In order to represent the wavelength dependence of polarization from IR to UV, Martin *et al.* (1999) suggested a five-parameter interpolation formula consisting of two terms describing UV and IR polarization

$$P(\lambda)/P_{\max} = P_{\mathrm{IR}}(\lambda)\mathcal{S} + P_{\mathrm{UV}}(\lambda)(1 - \mathcal{S}), \qquad (3.49)$$

where

$$P_{\mathrm{IR}}(\lambda) = (\lambda_{\max}/\lambda)^{\hat{\beta}} \exp\left\{ \hat{\beta}/\hat{\delta} \left[1 - (\lambda_{\max}/\lambda)^{\hat{\delta}} \right] \right\}, \qquad (3.50)$$

$$P_{\mathrm{UV}}(\lambda) = \exp[-\hat{\alpha}\ln^2(\lambda_{\max}/\lambda)], \qquad (3.51)$$

and

$$\mathcal{S} = \frac{1}{1 + (\lambda_{\max}/\lambda)^{\hat{\gamma}}}. \qquad (3.52)$$

The value of $\hat{\gamma}$ is equal to 4 for stars with $\lambda_{\max} \approx 0.55\,\mu$m. The parameters $P_{\max}$ and $\lambda_{\max}$ are determined from fitting Serkowski's curve in the visible. The parameter $\hat{\alpha}$ ought to be close to K_{UV} (see Eq. (3.48)), and the power-law index $\hat{\beta}$ to be near 2. The fifth free parameter is the power $\hat{\delta}$.

Variations of the polarizing efficiency in cold dark clouds and starforming regions are of special interest. It was found that in several dark clouds: L 1755, L 1506, B 216–217 (Goodman *et al.*, 1995; Arce *et al.*, 1998) the rise of polarization with growing extinction is stopped beginning at some value of A_{V}. Such a break in the P–A_{V} relation at extinction of $1^{\mathrm{m}}3 \pm 0^{\mathrm{m}}2$ was detected in cold dense regions in Taurus (Arce *et al.*, 1998). The results obtained are shown in Fig. 33. The difference in the polarizing efficiency of dark cloud and warm ISM is clearly seen. This fact may have different explanations. The effectiveness of grain alignment may drop in dark clouds (Lazarian *et al.*, 1997), but it is possible to propound a dozen other factors influencing the polarization degree. They are discussed qualitatively by Goodman *et al.* (1995; see their Table 4). Some trends in variations of polarization following from the optics of non-spherical particles are considered in Sect. 3.4.

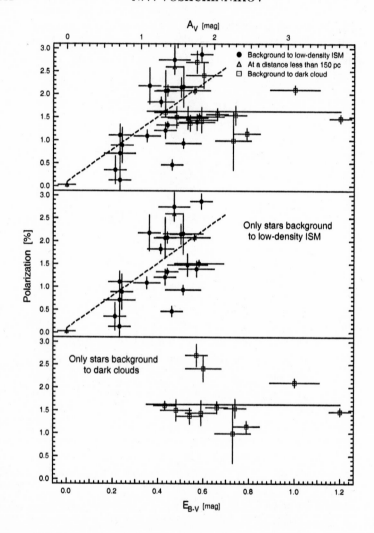

Figure 33 Observed variations of polarization with extinction for stars in Taurus ($A_V = 3.1E(B - V)$). The dashed line gives the least-square fit for stars background to the low-density ISM: $P = 3.58E(B - V) + 0.09$. The solid line shows the same for stars background to dark clouds: $P = 0.03E(B - V) + 1.61$. After Arce *et al.* (1998).

3.3.2 Circular polarization

The idea that the dichroism of interstellar space is accompanied by birefringence was suggested by van de Hulst (1957) in the last page of his book. This can lead to appearance of the noticeable *circular polarization* in the direction of a source with strong linear polarization (like Crab nebula) if the directions of the linear polarization in the source and foreground dust cloud differ by 45°. Fifteen years later Martin *et al.* (1972) discovered the interstellar circular polarization in the direction of Crab nebula. At the same time, Kemp and Wolstencroft (1972) published the data on circular polarization for six stars. As a rule, the degree of circular polarization is very small ($q_c(\lambda) \lesssim 0.02\%$; Martin and Campbell, 1976) and its sign changes at some wavelength λ_c. Martin and Angel (1976) investigated the dependence $q_c(\lambda)$ for six stars and found that the change of sign occurred near the wavelength where the linear polarization reached a maximum, i.e., $\lambda_c \approx \lambda_{max}$. It was also noted that circular polarization is observed for stars showing changes of the positional angle of linear polarization with wavelength (Martin, 1974).

Martin (1975) established a semi-empirical relation between linear dichroism and linear birefringence (i.e. between $P(\lambda)$ and $q_c(\lambda)$), while Shapiro (1975) showed that they were uniquely connected by a Kramers–Kronig integral relations (see Sect. 2.1.2). After the development of UV and IR polarimetry, interest in observations of interstellar circular polarization vanished although the problems with its explanation have not been solved (see Sect. 3.4.3).

3.3.3 Large-scale polarization in the Galaxy

In the 1970s, the optical polarization observations of several thousand stars have been accumulated. Then a possibility of studying structure of the galactic magnetic field using starlight polarization came into existence. For this, the distribution of "polarization vectors" (bars giving P and θ_G for separate stars) is mapped out in the galactic coordinates. Early investigations already showed that polarization vectors had a rather uniform alignment parallel to the galactic plane

N.V. VOSHCHINNIKOV

in certain directions and a disorder in other directions (see discussion in Serkowski, 1973; Martin, 1978; Whittet, 1992).

Heiles (2000) compiled the data on interstellar linear polarization from available polarization catalogs. As a result, new catalog containing information on the position, polarization[23], colour excess $E(B - V)$, distance, etc. of 9286 stars has been created. These data were statistically analysed by Fosalba *et al.* (2002a, 2002b) who selected 5513 stars with small absolute error in the polarization degree ($< 0.25\%$) and positive extinction.

Figure 34 shows the polarization map for a subsample of stars chosen by Fosalba *et al.* (2002a, 2002b). Practically all high latitude ($|b| > 10°$) stars are nearby ($D < 1$ kpc). Within the galactic plane one can find relatively distant stars, though the vast majority are within 2 kpc.

Fosalba *et al.* (2002b) note that the polarization degree and colour excess grow linearly with distance up to $D \approx 2$ kpc. Beyond ~ 2 kpc, stars have roughly constant values for both quantities: $P \approx 2\%$ and $E(B - V) \approx 0\overset{m}{.}6$. The overall behaviour of P and $E(B - V)$ with distance was fitted by third-order polynomials up to $D \approx 6$ kpc

$$P \approx 0.13 + 1.81D - 0.47D^2 + 0.036D^3 \%, \qquad (3.53)$$

$$E(B - V) \approx 0.08 + 0.5D - 0.135D^2 + 0.0104D^3. \qquad (3.54)$$

For stars with $E(B - V) \lesssim 1\overset{m}{.}0$, the relation between polarization degree and colour excess is close to the linear one

$$P \approx 3.5 \, E(B - V)^{0.8} \%, \qquad (3.55)$$

which is much smaller than the observational upper limit given by Eq. (3.44).

The dependence of polarization on the galactic coordinates is obtained similar to that found earlier. After averaging of the data over $10°$ longitude bins, both the polarization degree and the normalized Stokes parameter q ($q = Q/I = P \cos 2(\theta_G - 90°)$) exhibit a sinusoidal-like variation with longitude with a $180°$ periodicity

---

[23] The polarization is given for one wavelength which is not specified but usually is in the visible part of the spectrum. The catalog can be obtained via anonymous ftp (see Sect. 5.2).

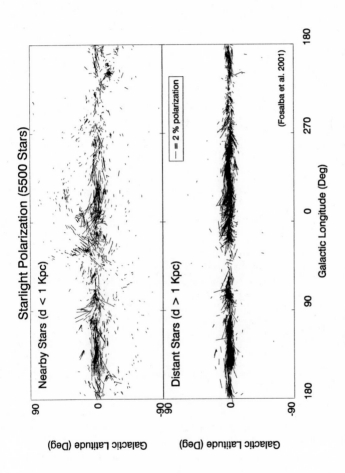

Figure 34 Starlight polarization vectors in the galactic coordinates for a sample of 5513 stars. For nearby stars (upper panel), the polarization is mainly produced in single local clouds, while the lower panel displays polarization averaged over many clouds in the galactic plane. The length of the vectors is proportional to the polarization degree and the scale used is shown in the lower panel. After Fosalba et al. (2002a).

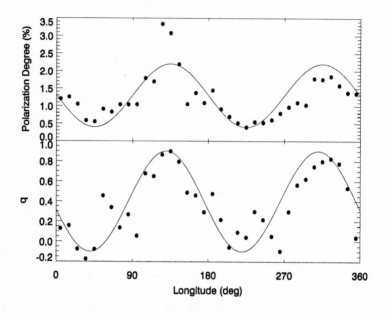

Figure 35 Starlight polarization degree (upper panel) and the normalized Stokes parameter q (lower panel) for data averaged in $10°$ longitude bins. The solid line shows a best fit to a sinusoidal dependence (see Eqs. (3.56) and (3.57)). After Fosalba *et al.* (2002b).

$$P \approx 1.3 + 0.9 \sin(2l + 180°) \%, \qquad (3.56)$$

$$q \approx 0.4 + 0.5 \sin(2l + 190°). \qquad (3.57)$$

These dependencies are plotted in Fig. 35 together with the observational data. The minimum values of q were found at galactic longitudes $l \approx 50°$ and $l \approx 230°$ whereas the maximum ones were determined at $l \approx 140°$ and $l \approx 320°$. This is in agreement with the previous results.

Only 25% of stars in the sample studied by Fosalba *et al.* (2002b) are located at high galactic latitudes ($|b| > 10°$). The data averaged over $10°$ latitude bins shows a strong dependence of the polarization degree with latitude. Its behaviour can be well described by a cosecant law

$$P \approx 0.1 + \frac{0.0067}{\sin(0.05|b|)} \%. \tag{3.58}$$

3.4   Interstellar polarization: interpretation

To model the interstellar polarization one needs to calculate the forward-transmitted radiation for an ensemble of non-spherical aligned dust grains. This procedure consists of two steps: 1) computations of the extinction cross-sections for two polarization modes and 2) averaging of cross-sections for given particles size and orientation distributions. Although the average cross-sections should be compared with observations, behaviour of the polarization cross-sections and efficiency of the alignment mechanisms are often analysed separately.

Let non-polarized stellar radiation passes through a dusty cloud with a homogeneous magnetic field. As follows from observations and theoretical considerations (Dolginov *et al.*, 1979), the *magnetic field determines the direction of alignment of dust grains*. The angle between the line of sight and the magnetic field is Ω ($0° \leq \Omega \leq 90°$). The linear polarization produced by a rotating single-size spheroidal particle is

$$P(\lambda) = \int_{\varphi', \omega', \beta'} \frac{1}{2} \left[C_{\text{ext}}^{\text{TM}}(m, r_V, \lambda, a/b, \alpha) - C_{\text{ext}}^{\text{TE}}(m, r_V, \lambda, a/b, \alpha) \right]$$

$$\times \hat{f}[\xi(r_V, \chi'', n_{\text{H}}, B, T_{\text{d}}, T_{\text{g}}), \beta'] \cos 2\psi \, d[\varphi', \omega', \beta'] \cdot N_{\text{d}} \cdot 100\%, \tag{3.59}$$

where $C_{\text{ext}}^{\text{TM, TE}}$ are the extinction cross-sections for two polarization modes (Sect. 2.2.1), N_{d} the column density of dust grains. The particles are assumed to be partially aligned: the major axis of the particle rotates in the spinning plane (φ' is the spin angle) which is perpendicular to the angular momentum $\vec{J}$. $\vec{J}$ spins (precesses) around the direction of magnetic field (ω' is the precession angle), β' is the precession-cone angle for $\vec{J}$. This is the imperfect Davies–Greenstein (IDG) orientation described by the function $\hat{f}(\xi, \beta')$ which depends on the alignment parameter ξ and the angle β'.

Note that the problem of grain alignment is one of the most difficult in the physics of cosmic dust. Here, the interaction of solid particles with gas, radiation and magnetic field is deeply intertwined. Davies and Greenstein (1951) assumed that Fe atoms embedded in dielectric particles gave them paramagnetic properties and opened the possibility of interaction with a weak interstellar magnetic field. The required orientation arises as a result of the effect of paramagnetic relaxation of thermally rotating grains. The Davies–Greenstein mechanism was further developed by Jones and Spitzer (1967) who obtained expressions for the distribution of angular momentum. In the simplest case, it is

$$\hat{f}(\xi, \beta') = \frac{\xi \sin \beta'}{(\xi^2 \cos^2 \beta' + \sin^2 \beta')^{3/2}}. \tag{3.60}$$

The parameter ξ is a function of the particle size r_V, the imaginary part of the grain magnetic susceptibility χ'' ($= \varkappa \omega_d / T_d$, where ω_d is the angular velocity of grain), gas density n_g, the strength of magnetic field B and dust (T_d) and gas (T_g) temperatures

$$\xi^2 = \frac{r_V + \delta_0(T_d/T_g)}{r_V + \delta_0}, \tag{3.61}$$

where

$$\delta_0^{\mathrm{IDG}} = 8.23\,10^{23} \frac{\varkappa B^2}{n_g T_g^{1/2} T_d}\,\mu\mathrm{m}. \tag{3.62}$$

The angle ψ in Eq. (3.59) is expressed via the angles $\varphi', \omega', \beta'$ and Ω, α (for definitions of the angles and relations between them see, for example, Hong and Greenberg, 1980 or Voshchinnikov, 1989). If the grains are not aligned $\xi = 1$ and $\hat{f}(\xi, \beta') = \sin \beta'$; in the case of the PDG $\xi = 0$ and $\hat{f}(\xi, \beta') = \delta(\beta')$[24].

Rotation is an important factor of any grain alignment mechanism. The faster it is the more effective the grain alignment should

---

[24] $\delta(z)$ is delta function.

be. The Davies–Greenstein mechanism considers thermally rotating grains. Purcell (1979) suggested a mechanism of supra-thermal spin alignment (SSA; "pinwheel" mechanism) where the grains were spun up to very high velocities as a result of the desorption of H_2 molecules from their surfaces. In this case, the alignment function is described by Eq. (3.60) but the parameter δ_0 is

$$\delta_0^{SSA} \approx 0.13(1 + 0.56/r_V)\delta_0^{IDG}, \qquad (3.63)$$

where r_V is in μm. Rotation can also arise due to radiation torques when "helical" grains scatter left- and right-circularly polarized light in a different way (Dolginov *et al.*, 1979; Draine and Weingartner, 1996; 1997; Weingartner and Draine, 2003), which can lead to the grain alignment in anisotropic radiation field. Alignment of thermally rotating grains is also possible by supersonic flows or Alfvénic waves or ambipolar diffusion. This so-called Gold-type[25] or mechanical alignment was generalized for supra-thermally rotating grains by Lazarian (1995). Note that some mechanisms can produce alignment when the major grain axes tend to align parallel to the magnetic field. Such an orientation is "wrong" for interstellar polarization but the mechanism may be "right" and operate in other conditions, for example in jets from YSO.

The development and current status of the major alignment mechanisms and principal physical processes forming their basis are reviewed by Roberge (1996), Lazarian *et al.* (1997), Lazarian (2000, 2003) and Draine (2003b). Unfortunately, the astrophysical significance of different alignment mechanisms remains unclear. This is connected, in particular, with very rough theoretical estimates of the polarization efficiency when instead of an alignment function like that given by Eq. (3.60) the Rayleigh reduction factor (see Greenberg, 1968) is used (e.g., Lazarian *et al.*, 1997).

The circular polarization is proportional to the product

$$q_c(\lambda) \propto \langle C_q(\lambda) \rangle_2 P_1(\lambda), \qquad (3.64)$$

where $\langle C_q(\lambda) \rangle$ is the average cross-section of circular polarization. The cross-section $C_q(\lambda)$ is calculated as the difference of phase lags

---

[25] Its idea was first suggested by Gold (1952).

$C_p^{\mathrm{TM}} - C_p^{\mathrm{TE}}$ represented by the imaginary parts of the corresponding complex extinction cross-sections. The circular polarization arises when the radiation linearly polarized in cloud "1" passes through cloud "2" (note the indices in Eq. (3.64)). Cloud "1" works as a linear polarizer and cloud "2" as a linear retarder (see Fig. 36). In such an optical device, the maximum transformation of the linear polarization to the circular one occurs when the optical axes of components are inclined by 45° in the plane perpendicular to the direction of light propagation (e.g., Tinbergen, 1996).

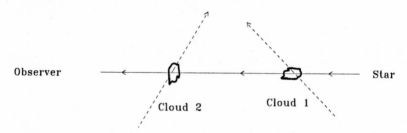

Figure 36 Scheme of the origin of the interstellar circular polarization. The dashed arrows show the direction of magnetic field in two clouds as is viewed from the side.

For simplicity, non-rotating particles of the same orientation are frequently considered. In this case of "picket fence" (PF) orientation, there are no integrals over angles φ', ω' and β' in Eq. (3.59). The polarization degree is proportional to the polarization cross-section $P(\lambda) \propto C_{\mathrm{pol}} = 1/2[C_{\mathrm{ext}}^{\mathrm{TM}}(\Omega) - C_{\mathrm{ext}}^{\mathrm{TE}}(\Omega)]$, where $\Omega = \alpha$. The dichroic polarization efficiency is defined by the ratio of the polarization cross-section (factor) to the extinction one

$$\frac{P(\lambda)}{\tau(\lambda)} = \pm\frac{C_{\mathrm{pol}}}{C_{\mathrm{ext}}} = \pm\frac{C_{\mathrm{ext}}^{\mathrm{TM}} - C_{\mathrm{ext}}^{\mathrm{TE}}}{C_{\mathrm{ext}}^{\mathrm{TM}} + C_{\mathrm{ext}}^{\mathrm{TE}}} \cdot 100\% = \pm\frac{Q_{\mathrm{ext}}^{\mathrm{TM}} - Q_{\mathrm{ext}}^{\mathrm{TE}}}{Q_{\mathrm{ext}}^{\mathrm{TM}} + Q_{\mathrm{ext}}^{\mathrm{TE}}} \cdot 100\%,$$

(3.65)

where the upper (lower) sign is related to prolate (oblate) spheroids. This ratio describes the efficiency of polarization of the initially non-polarized light transmitted through an uniform slab consisting of non-rotating particles of the same orientation.

A more complicated case is the *perfect rotational (2D) orientation* (or perfect Davies–Greenstein orientation, PDG) when the major axis of a non-spherical particle lies in the same plane at all times. For the 2D orientation, integration is performed over the spin angle φ' only. This gives for prolate spheroids

$$P(\Omega) = \frac{2}{\pi} \int_0^{\pi/2} C_{\mathrm{pol}}(\alpha) \, \cos 2\psi \, d\varphi' \cdot N_{\mathrm{d}} \cdot 100\%, \qquad (3.66)$$

where the angle α is connected with Ω and φ' ($\cos\alpha = \sin\Omega\cos\varphi'$). For oblate spheroids randomly aligned in a plane, we have $\Omega = \alpha$ and

$$P(\Omega) = C_{\mathrm{pol}}(\Omega) \cdot N_{\mathrm{d}} \cdot 100\%. \qquad (3.67)$$

As a result, the expected polarization will be determined by:

- the particle refractive index, size and shape via the polarization cross-section C_{pol};

- the relation between the strength of the magnetic field, gas and dust temperature, gas density, etc. via the alignment function $\hat{f}(\xi, \beta')$;

- the direction of alignment depending on the angle Ω (or α) via both C_{pol} and $\hat{f}(\xi, \beta')$.

The simplest types of orientations like PF or PDG allow one to investigate the influence of the first and third factors. The dependence of P on N_{d} is excluded because the normalized polarization or polarization efficiency is usually studied.

3.4.1   Polarization efficiency: size/shape/orientation effects

The behaviour of the polarization efficiency P/τ (see Eq. (3.65)) for non-absorbing and absorbing spheroids is shown in Fig. 37 for the case when a maximum polarization is expected (PF alignment, $\alpha = 90°$). The chosen refractive indices are typical of water ice and soot. The size/shape dependence of the ratio P/τ for these two materials is different. The polarization efficiency grows with the aspect ratio a/b

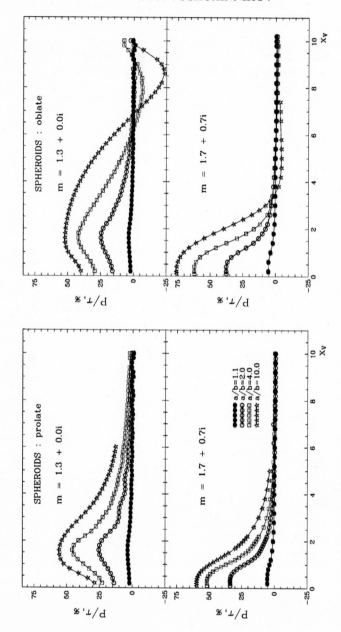

Figure 37 Polarization efficiency against x_V for prolate and oblate spheroids with $m = 1.3 + 0.0i$ and $1.7 + 0.7i$, picket fence orientation, $\alpha = 90°$. The size/shape effects are illustrated. After Voshchinnikov *et al.* (2000).

and is larger for oblate particles in comparison with prolate ones of the same volume but the polarization reversal takes place for disk-like particles. The last effect depends on the imaginary part of the refractive index and appears for absorbing prolate particles of large sizes as well.

In Table 11, the values of the parameter $x_V = 2\pi r_V/\lambda$ at which the polarization cross section $C_{pol}/\pi r_V^2$ reaches a maximum are presented for icy particles at $\alpha = 90°$. These values (x_V^{pol}) were obtained without smoothing the curves of $C_{pol}/\pi r_V^2(x_V)$. From Table 11, one

Table 11 Values of $x_V = 2\pi r_V/\lambda$ at which the circular polarization changes sign (x_V^c) and the linear polarization cross-section peaks (x_V^{pol}) for spheroids and infinitely long circular cylinders with $m = 1.31 + 0.01i$ and $\alpha = 90°$. Adapted from Voshchinnikov (1990).

a/b	x_V^{pol}	$\dfrac{C_{pol}}{\pi r_V^2}$	$\dfrac{Q_{pol}}{Q_{ext}}$	r_V^{pol*}, μm	s^{**}, μm	x_V^c	$\dfrac{x_V^c}{x_V^{pol}}$
			Prolate spheroid				
1.5	3.45	0.1036	0.057	0.30	0.26	3.40	0.99
2.0	3.44	0.1536	0.092	0.30	0.23	3.41	0.99
3.0	3.15	0.2036	0.157	0.28	0.19	3.42	1.08
5.0	3.71	0.3510	0.241	0.32	0.19	3.76	1.01
∞^{***}	1.94	0.3552	0.184	—	0.19	2.00	1.03
			Oblate spheroid				
1.5	3.05	0.1210	0.067	0.27	0.31	2.97	0.97
2.0	3.01	0.2237	0.124	0.26	0.34	3.05	1.01
3.0	3.39	0.4052	0.176	0.30	0.43	3.38	1.00
5.0	3.34	0.6342	0.298	0.29	0.50	3.41	1.02

$^*r_V^{pol}$ is the radius of equivolume sphere corresponding to x_V^{pol} if $\lambda = \lambda_{max} = 0.55\,\mu$m; $^{**}s = b$ for prolate spheroids and $s = a$ for oblate spheroids; *** For infinitely long cylinders the following quantities are given: the parameter $x_{cyl}^{pol} = 2\pi r_{cyl}/\lambda$ corresponding to the maximum linear polarization cross-section $Q_{ext}^E - Q_{ext}^H$, polarizing efficiency, the cylinder radius r_{cyl} for $\lambda = 0.55\,\mu$m multiplied by the factor 1.145 (see Sect. 3.2.1), the parameter x_{cyl}^c at which the circular polarization changes the sign, and the ratio x_{cyl}^c/x_{cyl}^{pol}.

can see that the growth of a/b leads to an increase of the polarization cross-sections and the polarizing efficiency of the medium, but the particle volume does not change strongly. With increasing a/b, the optical properties of prolate spheroids and infinitely long cylinders become similar.

It is also seen from Fig. 37 that relatively large particles produce *no polarization* independently of their shape. For absorbing particles, it occurs at smaller x_V values than for non-absorbing ones. However, the position at which the ratio P/τ peaks is rather stable in every panel of Fig. 37 independently of a/b.

This effect is broken if one considers tilted radiation incidence (Figs. 38, 39). The angular dependence of the extinction and linear polarization factors in Eq. (3.65) differs: if α decreases, the position of the maximum for Q_{ext} shifts to smaller values of x_V while that for Q_{pol} shifts to larger x_V (Fig. 38, upper panels). As a result, the maximum polarization efficiency for prolate spheroids occurs for smaller x_V in the case of tilted orientation (Fig. 38, lower left panel). And the picture is reversed for oblate particles (see Fig. 39).

Thus, it should be emphasized that for particles larger than the radiation wavelength, the linear polarization is expected to be rather small. This does not allow one to distinguish between the particle properties like refractive index, shape, orientation. Even in the case of ideal (PF) orientation, large particles (possibly available in dark clouds, see Fig. 33 and discussion in Sect. 3.3.1) do not polarize the transmitted radiation. So, the decrease of the ratio P/A_V with the rise of R_V like found by Clayton and Cardelli (1988) should imply only that large grains are not efficient at producing polarization and is not connected with the change of grain shape or their less efficient alignment.

At the same time, there is a possibility of reducing of the polarization efficiency associated with growth of the spherical icy mantles on non-spherical cores in dark clouds. In Fig. 40, this effect is illustrated for spheroidal particles with astrosil core and water ice mantle. The influence of variations of the mantle shape for particles of different sizes is shown. The shape of the core was fixed and for each curve the shape of the mantle remains the same. In this case, the ratio of the core volume to that of the particle does not change (see Farafonov *et al.*, 1996). For the values of a/b(core) used, it is rather small (from

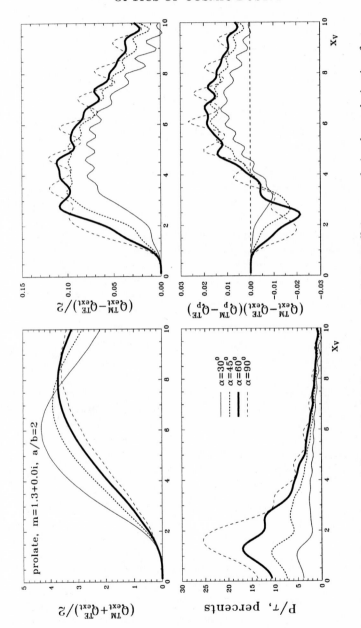

Figure 38 Extinction and linear polarization factors, polarization efficiency and circular polarization factors against x_V for prolate spheroids with $m = 1.3 + 0.0i$ and $a/b = 2$, picket fence orientation. The effect of variations of particle orientation is illustrated.

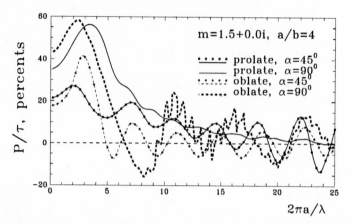

Figure 39 Polarization efficiency as a function of the size parameter $2\pi a/\lambda$ for the prolate and oblate homogeneous spheroids with $m = 1.5 + 0.0i$ and $a/b = 4$. The behaviour of extinction efficiencies is shown in Fig. 21. The effect of variations of particle orientation is illustrated.

0.11 to 0.004) and, therefore, the core's influence appears for particles of small radii only. For particles larger than $\sim 0.05\,\mu$m, the polarization seems to be mainly determined by the shape of the particle mantle.

Values of the ratio P/τ presented in Figs. 37–40 are usually much larger than the upper limit for the interstellar polarization given by Eq. (3.44): $P_{\max}/\tau = P_{\max}/E(\mathrm{B} - \mathrm{V})\cdot 1.086/R_{\mathrm{V}} \lesssim 3.2\%$. In order to reduce the ratio P/τ, the imperfect orientation of dust grains should be considered. Note that the PDG orientation (in comparison with PF) should decrease the polarization of prolate grains only as PF and PDG orientations for oblate grains are equivalent (see Eq. (3.67)). It is interesting that the polarization efficiency created by rotating ellipsoidal particles is lower than that of oblate spheroids and sometimes even prolate spheroids (Fig. 41)[26]. Taking into account the problems with grain alignment in dark clouds (e.g., Lazarian et al., 1997), the hope to solve the problem of the origin of polarization with the aid of more complex three-dimensional particles looks like unfounded.

---

[26] A similar conclusion follows from calculations made by Matsumura and Seki (1996).

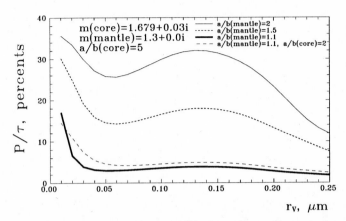

Figure 40 Polarization efficiency as a function of particle equivolume radius r_V for prolate core-mantle spheroids with $m(\text{core}) = 1.679 + 0.03i$ and $m(\text{mantle}) = 1.3 + 0.0i$, PF orientation, $\alpha = 90°$. The effect of variations of mantle shape is illustrated.

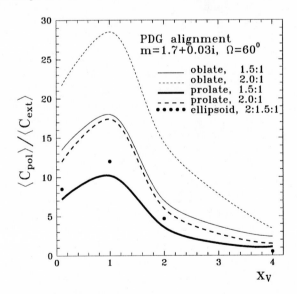

Figure 41 Polarization efficiency as a function of size parameter x_V for prolate and oblate spheroids and ellipsoids with $m = 1.70 + 0.03i$, PDG orientation, $\Omega = 60°$. The effect of variations of particle shape is illustrated. Adapted from Il'in *et al.* (2003).

3.4.2   Linear polarization: wavelength dependence

Fitting the observed dependence $P(\lambda)$ includes calculations of the polarization cross-sections $\langle C_{pol}(\lambda) \rangle$ averaged over particles orientation and size distribution, their normalization and the comparison of obtained dependencies $P(\lambda)/P_{max}(\lambda_{max}/\lambda)$ with Serkowski's curve representing observational data for a chosen star. Here, only two parameters of the observed polarization are considered: the wavelength at which the polarization reaches a maximum, λ_{max}, and the width of the polarization curve W related to the parameter K of Serkowski's curve (Eq. (3.45)). Thus, the absolute value of polarization is neglected.

Variations of the polarization factors with wavelength are shown in Fig. 42 for homogeneous spheroidal particles with PF orientation. The Figure illustrates how changes of the chemical composition, particle size, shape and orientation influence the polarization factors. The distinction between prolate and oblate spheroids is also clearly seen. In particular, oblate particles polarize radiation more efficiently than prolate ones. From Fig. 42, it is possible to estimate approximately the dependence of λ_{max} on particle parameters. λ_{max} shifts to longer wavelengths (λ^{-1} decreases) if the particle size r_V grows, the aspect ratio a/b becomes smaller and the inclination (angle α) increases (prolate spheroids) or decreases (oblate spheroids). The use of more absorbing particles (Fig. 42, upper left panel) also leads to a shift of λ_{max} to the IR wavelengths. Note that the maximum polarization occurs at shorter wavelengths for oblate spheroids in comparison with prolate spheroids having the same parameters.

As a result, one can easily find an ensemble of particles with a combination of parameters which reproduce the position of the maximum on the polarization curve. Unfortunately, to adjust another parameter — the width of polarization curve — is a more difficult problem: the theoretical curves are narrower than the observed ones. This is seen from Fig. 43 where the normalized polarization factors from Fig. 42 are compared with Serkowski's curves calculated using Eqs. (3.43) and (3.47). The curve with $\lambda_{max} = 0.55\,\mu$m is noticeably wider than the theoretical curve. Only by increasing λ_{max} (say up to $1\,\mu$m which leads to the decrease of W) can the width of the polarization curve be reproduced. However, the position of the maximum for theoretical factors occurs at smaller wavelengths than $1\,\mu$m (Fig. 42).

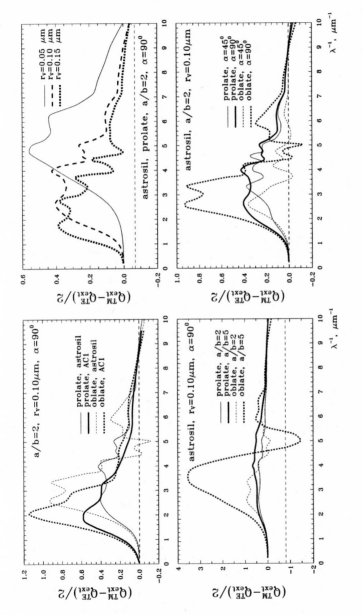

Figure 42 Wavelength dependence of the polarization factors for homogeneous spheroids consisting of astrosil and amorphous carbon. The effect of variations of particle size, shape and orientation is illustrated.

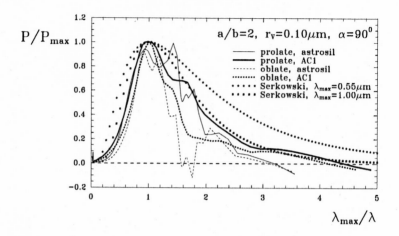

Figure 43 Normalized polarization factors for homogeneous spheroids consisting of astrosil and amorphous carbon as a function of λ_{max}/λ. Serkowski's curves were calculated using Eqs. (3.43) and (3.47).

Il'in and Henning (2003) have performed extensive calculations of interstellar polarization for polydisperse ensembles of spheroidal particles with a shape distribution. They found that the profile of the polarization curve mainly determined by oblate spheroids was always narrower than the observed one. Prolate spheroids alone can produce the polarization curves nearly as wide as observed but they are very blueshifted compared with the observed curves. Note also that the increase of W occurs if the direction of grain alignment deviates from normal to the line of sight (i.e. $\Omega < 90°$; Voshchinnikov et al., 1986; Voshchinnikov, 1989; Il'in and Henning, 2003).

Very likely, it is better to compare the theoretical polarization efficiencies with observations than normalized polarization given by Serkowski's curve. This allows one to include extinction into consideration and comprehend grain alignment efficiency in a full manner. The wavelength dependencies of the polarization efficiency for particles with the same parameters as in Fig. 42 are plotted in Fig. 44. Variations of the ratio P/τ with the particle parameters are similar to those discussed in Sect. 3.4.1: the ratio grows with an increase of

a/b and α (Ω) and is as a rule larger for oblate spheroids than for prolate ones. The use of more absorbing particles (e.g. of amorphous carbon) leads to an increase of polarization in the red part of the spectrum ($\lambda \gtrsim 0.5\,\mu$m, Fig. 44, upper left panel). The maximum of the polarization efficiency strongly shifts with a change of particle radius (Fig. 44, upper right panel) but approximately corresponds to the close values of x_V as is shown in Fig. 37.

The presentation of the observational data in the form of the wavelength dependence of the polarization efficiency is traditionally not performed. However, Whittet (1996b) in Fig. 9 shows the normalized dependence $P(\lambda)/A(\lambda) \cdot A_V/P_{\max}$ for five stars in the wavelength range $\lambda^{-1} \approx 0.2$–$8\,\mu$m^{-1}. In the visible and near UV ($\lambda^{-1} \approx 1.8$–$3\,\mu$m^{-1}), these dependencies are quite similar for all stars and their variations with wavelength may be approximated as $\lambda^{1.60}$. The dashed segment in Fig. 44 represents this "observational" dependence.

The angular dependence of the polarization factors and polarization efficiencies gives a possibility of concluding that there should exist anticorrelation in variations of P/τ and $\lambda_{\max}$. The smaller α (or Ω) is, the smaller the polarization efficiency and the larger $\lambda_{\max}$ should be. Such a tendency can be displayed as a relation between $P_{\max}/E(B - V)$ and $\lambda_{\max}$ for stars located in different galactic directions and seen through single dust clouds. Apparently, such a dependence exists for stars with distances $D \lesssim 1\,$kpc located in the galactic plane (see Voshchinnikov, 1989). It can be used for diagnostics of the inclination of the magnetic field to the line of sight where the directions with large $\lambda_{\max}$ and small $P_{\max}/E(B - V)$ can be attributed to the small values of the angle Ω, i.e. here the magnetic field is nearly parallel to the line of sight.

3.4.3   Circular polarization: change of sign

Traditionally, the main problem considered in connection with circular interstellar polarization is the meaning of the wavelength where $q_c(\lambda)$ changes the sign λ_c. Its proximity to $\lambda_{\max}$ is treated as the indicator of the dielectric nature of interstellar grains (see, e.g., Whittet, 2003). This feature was established by Martin (1972) in the

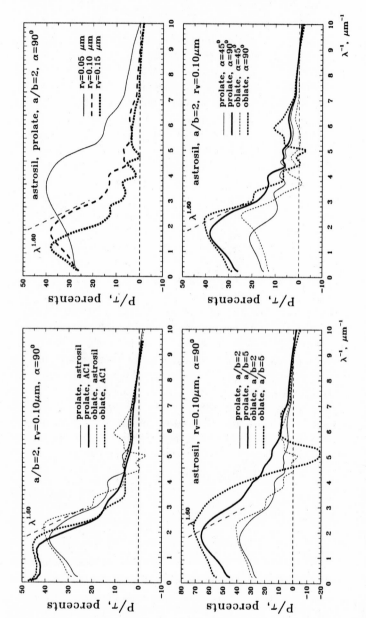

Figure 44 Wavelength dependence of the polarization efficiency for homogeneous spheroids consisting of astrosil and amorphous carbon. The effect of variations of the particle size, shape and orientation is illustrated. The dashed segment shows the approximate wavelength dependence of P/τ at optical wavelengths for five stars as reported by Whittet (1996b).

first serious theoretical paper which accompanied the discovery of interstellar circular polarization. Martin (1972, 1974) found that the condition $\lambda_c \approx \lambda_{max}$ could be satisfied if the imaginary part of the refractive index was low at visible wavelengths ($k \lesssim 0.1$). However, Shapiro (1975) using DDA calculations for parallelepipeds of magnetite showed that a strongly absorbing conductor could reproduce this condition as well. Given conclusion is, possibly, not unquestionable because of doubt about the application of DDA to highly absorbing particles. Chlewicki and Greenberg (1990) reexamined the relationship between the interstellar linear and circular polarization on the basis of Kramers–Kronig relations. They concluded that the observed connection between λ_c and λ_{max} was reached independently of specific characteristics of grains, so long as they provided the "correct"[27] linear polarization. Note also that the shape effects for circular polarization were not analyzed: Martin (1972, 1974) considered infinite cylinders with PF orientation and $\alpha = 90°$, Chlewicki and Greenberg (1990) performed calculations for infinite cylinders with PDG and IDG orientations and $\Omega = 90°$.

Calculations made for spheroidal particles show that the position where the circular polarization changes the sign shifts with variations of the particle inclination in the same manner as the position of λ_{max}. This is clearly seen from Fig. 38 (right panels) where the efficiency factors are plotted for prolate spheroids with $a/b = 2$: reduction of α leads to increase of the x_V values where the circular polarization factors intersect the zero level. This means that the positions of both λ_c and λ_{max} should move to shorter wavelengths if the direction of alignment approaches the line of sight. Such a behaviour is evident from Fig. 45 (middle panel) for prolate spheroids while for oblate particles the displacement takes place in the opposite direction. Figure 45 (upper panel) also demonstrates changes of circular polarization with wavelength for particles of astrosil and AC1. Comparison with the corresponding picture for linear polarization (Fig. 42, upper left panel) enables to observe an approximate coincidence of λ_c and λ_{max} for both dielectric and absorbing particles (see also Figs. 10.18 and

---

[27] "Correctness" is contained in the use of the measured optical constants for which real and imaginary parts are already connected by Kramers–Kronig relations but not a wavelength-independent refractive index.

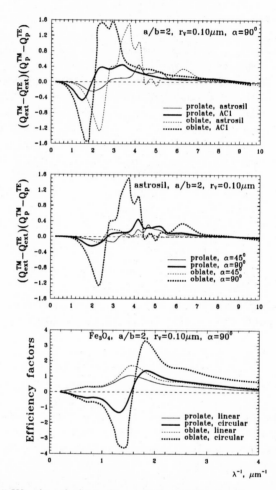

Figure 45 Wavelength dependence of the polarization factors for circular polarization. The corresponding factors for linear polarization are shown in Fig. 42 (upper and middle panels). On the lower panel, the wavelength dependence of the factors for linear $(Q_{ext}^{TM} - Q_{ext}^{TE})/2$ and circular $(Q_{ext}^{TM} - Q_{ext}^{TE})(Q_p^{TM} - Q_p^{TE})$ polarization for prolate and oblate spheroids of magnetite (Fe_3O_4) is shown. The effect of variations of particle composition and shape is illustrated.

10.19 in Krügel, 2003). This is also disclosed on Fig. 45 (lower panel) which displays the wavelength dependence of the factors of linear and circular polarization for particles of magnetite as was done by Shapiro (1975). We can confirm his conclusion about the proximity of λ_c and λ_{max} although the shape of curves for spheroids differs from that for parallelepipeds.

Finally, it can be concluded that *the wavelength where the interstellar circular polarization changes the sign and its coincidence with λ_{max} tell us almost nothing about the absorptive properties of interstellar grains but the wavelength dependence $q_c(\lambda)$ and in particular positions of the maxima/minima can serve for clearing up the dust properties.* It is important that from the point of view of circular polarization there exists a large difference between prolate and oblate grains. The latter particles always produce much larger polarization (Fig. 45). Note also that the circular polarization observed for stars is evidence of the twisted structure of interstellar magnetic fields in their directions and gives information on the *birefringence in the dust cloud nearest to the observer.*

3.4.4   Some steps in the modelling of polarization

Modelling of the interstellar polarization usually accompanies modelling of the interstellar extinction. Early models of Greenberg and Shah (1966) and Greenberg (1968) dealt with homogeneous cylindrical grains having the PF or PDG orientation.

The polarizing efficiency of non-absorbing spheroids of single size with PF orientation was considered by Martin (1978) and Rogers and Martin (1979).

Hong and Greenberg (1980) developed a unified model of interstellar grains which was applied to an explanation of interstellar extinction, linear and circular polarization. This model included partly aligned (IDG orientation) silicate core–ice mantle cylindrical particles and bare silicate and graphite spheres for an explanation of the UV extinction. The authors used the particle size distribution in the form given by Eq. (3.38). Aannestad and Greenberg (1983) expanded this model having included a modification of grain sizes by accretion and coagulation. The given refinement was directed on the explanation of the observed correlation between the width of the linear polarization curve and λ_{max}. Besides this, the efficiency of grain alignment in dark clouds was analyzed and it was shown that only Purcell's (1979) mechanism of SSA could be effective there. Unfortunately, to reduce the computational work Aannestad and Greenberg (1983) abandoned the integration over the precession angle ω' in Eq. (3.59) that led to considerable errors (Voshchinnikov, 1989).

A model with cylindrical grains analogous to that of Hong and Greenberg (1980) was worked out by Voshchinnikov et al. (1986) for the interpretation of interstellar extinction and polarization in the visible part of the spectrum. They established a detailed connection between the observed quantities and the model parameters, having paid special attention to their dependence on the orientation angle Ω. Il'in (1987) applied the model to the interpretation of the wavelength dependence of interstellar extinction, linear and circular polarization for the star HD 204827.

The MRN model (Mathis et al., 1977) with the power-law size distribution (Eq. (3.39)) was extended by Mathis (1979, 1986) to infinitely long cylinders for an explanation of the interstellar polarization. In the first work, the observed polarization was fitted assuming that only silicate grains above a certain size are aligned (PDG orientation). The power index was adopted to be smaller than that used for an explanation of interstellar extinction (2.5 instead of 3.5). Mathis (1986) suggested an extension of the Davis-Greenstein mechanism where rotating grains were assumed to be perfectly aligned if they contained at least one super-paramagnetic inclusion. Grains without inclusions were assumed to be randomly oriented in space (3D orientation).

The interstellar extinction and polarization curves for a polydisperse ensemble of homogeneous icy prolate spheroids with $a/b = 2$ were compared with those for infinite cylinders by Voshchinnikov (1990). The PDG, IDG and SSA alignment of particles was considered. It was found that the curves of interstellar linear polarization for cylinders and spheroids showed a resemblance, but the position of maximum seemed to shift to the red with an increase of the aspect ratio. Also, the curve $P(\lambda)/P_{max}$ for spheroids is slightly narrower than for cylinders.

Wolff *et al.* (1993) analyzed the applicability of three dust grain models to explain different types of the UV polarization curves (see Fig. 32). Spheroidal particles with the PDG orientation were used. Their optical properties were calculated with the DDA technique. It was shown that the MRN model with bare silicate grains could reproduce Serkowski's and super-Serkowski's behaviour of the polarization curves. Small aligned graphite disks were used in order to fit the polarization bump seen in HD 197770.

Using MEM, Kim and Martin (1994, 1995) reconstructed the size distribution of interstellar grains from the observed wavelength dependence of interstellar polarization. Infinite cylinders (Kim and Martin, 1994) and prolate/oblate spheroids (Kim and Martin, 1995) of astrosil with the PF or PDG orientation and $\alpha(\text{or}\,\Omega) = 90°$ were considered. The derived size distributions peak at mean size ~ 0.1–$0.2\,\mu$m. The exact form of $n(r)$ depends on the input parameters: the correspondingly selected optical constants and aspect ratio can reproduce Serkowski's curves with $\lambda_{\text{max}} = 0.52 - 0.68\,\mu$m.

Matsumura and Seki (1996) calculated the wavelength dependence of extinction and polarization in the IR for spheroidal and ellipsoidal particles composed of amorphous carbon and silicate. The optical properties of the particles were found on the basis of the Fredholm integral equation method. It was shown that the power law dependence of extinction and polarization in the IR could be reproduced if the particle size was $r_V \approx 0.1\,\mu$m.

A new "unified" model of interstellar dust was suggested by Li and Greenberg (1997). A treatment of linear and circular polarization was performed using the model of homogeneous finite cylinders with the PDG orientation and $\Omega = 90°$. However, the optical constants for particles were calculated using the Garnett rule as they consist of a silicate core and organic refractory mantle. This model was applied by Li and Greenberg (1998) for the interpretation of the extinction and polarization curves for the star HD 210121.

Wurm and Schnaiter (2002) calculated the linear polarization in the wavelength range $\lambda = 0.3$–$1.0\,\mu$m for aligned (PF orientation, $\Omega = 90°$) dust aggregates consisting of 4, 8, 16, 32 and 64 spherical particles (monomers). A power-law size distribution of monomers with the refractive index $m = 1.7 + 0.1i$ was considered. The calculations showed that the polarization efficiency decreased with increasing the aggregate size (monomer number per aggregate).

Summarizing, it should be stated that a modern model of interstellar polarization, including the recent achievements of light scattering theory and grain alignment study, remains to be developed.

4   SOME CONCLUSIONS

The state of art in dust modelling discussed above allows us to conclude that now there exist laboratory refractive indices of cosmic dust analogues, advanced light scattering theories and well-developed radiative transfer technique. All together they permit one to construct the complex models of dusty objects. *But the principle of optical equivalence introduced by George Gabriel Stokes does work!* This means that *we have only four Stokes parameters* I, Q, U, V *for comparison of the theory with observations.* Different models may give the same Stokes parameters and, therefore, *all models are ambiguous* to some degree.

Forward-transmitted radiation (interstellar extinction and polarization) discussed above is the main method for the investigation of cosmic dust grains but this method does not yield comprehensive information about the grain properties. However, in this case only the Stokes parameters I (extinction) and Q, V (linear, circular polarization) for one scattering angle ($\Theta = 0°$) are used. Additional information about cosmic dust would be expected to extract from the observations at several scattering angles and thermal dust emission. These topics will be analyzed in Part II. It contains the consideration of:

- scattered radiation;

- dust absorption/emission (continuum and bands);

- radiation pressure (and grain motion);

- dust properties in different objects from Solar System to very distant galaxies and quasars.

5 APPENDICES

5.1 List of abbreviations

2MASS — Two-Micron All-Sky Survey
AC — amorphous carbon
AFGL — Air Force Geophysical Laboratory
AGB — Asymptotic Giant Branch (type of stars)
AGN — active galactic nuclei
astrosil — astronomical silicate
COBE — COsmic Background Explorer
CS — circumstellar
DDA — discrete dipole approximation
DENIS — Deep Near Infrared Survey
DGL — diffuse galactic light
DIRBE — Diffuse Infrared Background Experiment
DOP — database of optical properties
EBCM — extended boundary conditions method
EEMA — extended effective medium approximation
EMT — effective medium theory
FUSE — Far Ultraviolet Spectroscopic Explorer
HG — Henyey–Greenstein (phase function)
HST —Hubble Space Telescope
IDG —imperfect Davies–Greenstein (orientation)
IR — infrared
IRAS — Infrared Astronomical Satellite
ISA — improved S-approximation
ISM — interstellar medium
ISO — Infrared Space Observatory
IUE — International Ultraviolet Explorer
JPDOC — Jena–Petersburg Database of Optical Constants
kpc — kiloparsec
LS — light scattering
MACHO — MAssive Compact Halo Objects;
mag — magnitude
MC — Monte Carlo
MEM — maximum entropy method
MoM — method of moments

MRN — Mathis–Rumpl–Nordsieck (dust mixture)
OAO — Orbiting Astronomical Observatory
OGLE — Optical Gravitational Lensing Experiment
OHM — Ossenkopf–Henning–Mathis (silicate material)
PAH — polycyclic aromatic hydrocarbons
PDG — perfect Davies–Greenstein (orientation)
PMS — pre-main-sequence
pc — parsec
ppm — parts per million
PROGRA^2 — PRopepriétés Optiques des GRains Astronomiques et
    Atmosphériques
RCB —(stars of type) R Coronae Borealis
RN — reflection nebula
SA — S-approximation
SED — Spectral Energy Distribution
SVM — separation of variables method
SSA — supra-thermal spin alignment
TD-1a — Thor-Delta (rocket system)
TMM — T-matrix method
UV — ultraviolet
WC — Wolf–Rayet (type of stars)
WUPPE — Wisconsin Ultraviolet Photo-Polarimeter Experiment
YSO — young stellar object

5.2   Dust in the Internet

Table 12 Some Internet resources related to the optics of cosmic dust.[*]

Resource	Author(s), Internet address
Optical properties:	
Jena–Petersburg Database of Optical Constants (JPDOC)	Th. Henning *et al.*, http://www.astro.uni-jena.de/Laboratory/Database/jpdoc/index.html

Table 12 (continued).

Resource	Author(s), Internet address
Microwave scattering experiments on cosmic dust analogues	B.Å.S. Gustafson, http://www.astro.ufl.edu/~gustaf/ facilities/microwave/ Microwave-lab-1.html
Light scattering experiments on cosmic dust analogues	J.W. Hovenier, H. Volten, http://www.astro.uva.nl/scatter
Optical properties of cosmic dust grains	B.T. Draine, http://astro.princeton.edu/~draine/ dust/dust.diel.html
Database of Optical Properties of dust particles (DOP)	V.B. Il'in *et al.*, http://www.astro.spbu.ru/DOP
Dust opacities	Th. Henning *et al.*, http://www.astro.uni-jena.de/Users/ dima/Opacities/opacities.html
Light scattering (LS) tools:	
SVM codes for spheres, cylinders, spheroids	N.V. Voshchinnikov, http://www.astro.spbu.ru/staff/ilin2/ SOFTWARE/
TMM codes for bispheres, cylinders, spheroids	M.I. Mishchenko, http://www.giss.nasa.gov/~crmim/ t_matrix.html
DDA code (DDScat)	B.T. Draine, ftp://astro.princeton.edu/~draine/ scat/DDSCAT.6.0.html
Collection of LS codes	Th. Wriedt, http://www.t-matrix.de
LS codes and references (SCATTERLIB)	P. Flatau, http://atol.ucsd.edu/~pflatau/ scatlib/
Library of LS software	http://emlib.jpl.nasa.gov
Optics on-line (partially commercial)	B. Michel, http://www.lightscattering.de/

Table 12 (continued).

Resource	Author(s), Internet address
Radiative transfer tools:	
1D code (DUSTY)	Ž. Ivezić *et al.*, http://www.pa.uky.edu/~moshe/dusty/
1–3D Monte-Carlo codes	S. Wolf, http://mc.caltech.edu/ swolf/mc3d/index.html
Intercomparison of 3D codes	http://climate.gsfc.nasa.gov/I3RC/
Interstellar extinction:	
Synthetic extinction curves	J.C. Weingartner, B.T. Draine, http://astro.princeton.edu/~draine/dust/dustmix.html
Extinction from the COBE/DIRBE maps	D.J. Schlegel *et al.*, http://www.astro.princeton.edu/~schlegel/dust/
Observed extinction curves	E.L. Fitzpatrick, ftp://astro2.ast.vill.edu/pub/fitz/Extinction/
Estimation of extinction in the Galaxy	R. Drimmel *et al.*, ftp://ftp.to.astro.it/astrometria/extinction/
Dust clouds in the Galaxy	C.M. Dutra, E. Bica, http://cdswww.u-strasbg.fr/cgi-bin/qcat?J/A+A/383/631/
Models of extinction in galaxies	S. Bianchi, A. Ferrara, http://www.arcetri.astro.it/ sbianchi/attenuation.html
Interstellar polarization:	
Polarization in the Galaxy	C. Heiles, ftp://vermi.berkeley.edu/pub/polcat/

Table 12 (continued).

Resource	Author(s), Internet address
Interstellar polarization survey	A.M. Magalhães *et al.*, http://www.astro.iag.usp.br/ ~antonio/survey/index_eng.htm
Interstellar polarization at high galactic latitudes	A.V. Berdyugin *et al.*, http://xml.gsfc.nasa.gov/archive/ journals/A+A/372/276/
Ground and space-based observations	http://www.sal.wisc.edu/WUPPE/ polcats/polcats.html

* The table was compiled by V.B. Il'in. It is also available at http://www.astro.spbu.ru/staff/ilin2/EDU/wwwdust.html.

5.3 Mie scattering by very large homogeneous spheres (numerical code)

The appendix contains the computer program that calculates the efficiency factors for a homogeneous sphere of practically unlimited size parameters. The widely used numerical code of Bohren and Huffman (1983) does not work for very large particles and cannot be extended to do that. Calculations of Shah (1992) are limited by the size parameter $x = 10^5$ where, in principle, the geometrical optics approximation should be applicable. However, his results show that for some factors this approximation gives only three significant digits. Possibly, such accuracy is enough for many applications but not for the backscattering factor for non-absorbing particles which cannot be expressed via the geometrical optics approximation (see Table 13).

Our computer code is written in FORTRAN 77 using double precision[28] and should be run both on personal computers and workstations. We calculate the Bessel functions of a real argument based on the upward recursion for the functions of the second kind, $Y_{n+1/2}(x)$,

---

[28] The program in FORTRAN 90 including the calculations of the scattering matrix for polydisperse mixtures of particles is available as well (see Wolf and Voshchinnikov, 2004 for details.)

which is known to be stable, the functions of the first kind, $J_{n+1/2}(x)$, are found from the relation for the product of the functions

$$J_{n+1/2}(x) = \left[\frac{2}{\pi x} + Y_{n+1/2}(x)J_{n-1/2}(x) \right] / Y_{n-1/2}(x). \qquad (5.1)$$

Equation (5.1) gives wrong results if $n \gg x$ but this is not the case of standard Mie calculations. In order to exclude the overflow in the forward recursion, a normalization is used. The description of the general method of calculations of Bessel functions can be found in Loskutov (1971).

The logarithmic derivative to the Bessel functions of a complex argument is calculated via the backward recursion. The starting number "num" for $x \leq 50000$ is chosen according to the recommendation of Loskutov (1971). It is smaller for large arguments than that given by Wiscombe (1980). The maximum size parameter to be reached is determined by the available computer memory capacity that is spent to keep the array for logarithmic derivatives values. In order to treat larger particles, one needs to enlarge the parameter "nterms".

The Mie series are terminated when the contribution of the n-th term to the extinction factor becomes smaller than $\epsilon = 10^{-15}$. Table 13, which is a continuation of Tables I–III of Shah (1992), gives benchmark results for two refractive indices. Note that the size parameter $x = 6\,283\,185.31$ corresponds to a particle with radius $r_s = 1$meter (!) at $\lambda = 1\,\mu$m.

```
c*NVVMIE.for ********************************************
c*NVVMIE * Light Scattering by Spherical Particles *****
c                                                       *
c  Calculations of extinction, scattering, absorption, *
c  etc. efficiency factors for homogeneous spheres      *
c  (Mie theory)                                         *
c......................................................*
c  Input data:            filename:  nvvmie.dat         *
c   ri = n+k*i: complex index of refraction             *
c           x1: minumum size                            *
c           dx: step over size                          *
c           x2: maximum size                            *
c......................................................*
```

```
c   Output data:              filename:  nvvmie.out          *
c   Qext : extinction factor                                *
c   Qsca : scattering factor                                *
c   Qabs : absorption factor                                *
c   Qbk   : backscattering factor                           *
c   Qpr   : radiation pressure factor                       *
c   albedo: albedo                                          *
c   g    : asymmetry factor                                 *
c.........................................................*
c NB! In order to treat very large particles,              *
c      one needs to enlarge the parameter NTERMS.          *
c.........................................................*
c created by N.V. Voshchinnikov                            *
c (c) 2001 Astronomical Institute, St. Petersburg Univ.*
c*****************************************************************
c
      implicit real*8(a-h,o-z)
      complex*16 ri
    1 format(3x,'SPHERES: homogeneous',/,
     *        3x,'THEORY:  exact')
    2 format(3x,'m = ',2F14.10,'*i')
    3 format(1x,91('.'))
    4 format(6x,'x',9x,'Qext',7x,'Qsca',7x,'Qabs',9x,
     *        'Qbk',11x,'Qpr',6x,'albedo',7x,'g')
    5 format(1x,91('-'))
    6 format(1x,F10.2,3(F11.6),f15.6,3(f11.5))
    7 format(2d14.10)
    8 format(d16.6)
c* input
      print *,'start nvvmie'
      open (unit=05,file='nvvmie.dat',status='old',
     *      access='sequential')
      open (unit=07,file='nvvmie.out',status='unknown',
     *      access='append')
      read (5,7) ri
      read (5,8) x1, dx, x2
      nx = (x2 - x1) / dx + 1
```

```
c*
      write (7,1)
      write (7,2) ri
      write (7,3)
      write (7,4)
      write (7,5)
c*  calculations
      do i = 1, nx
        x = x1 + dx * (i - 1)
        call shexqnn(ri, x, Qext, Qsca, Qabs, Qbk, Qpr,
     *               albedo, g, ier)
c*  output
        if (ier.eq.0) then
          write (7,6) x, Qext, Qsca, Qabs, Qbk, Qpr,
     *                albedo, g
          write (*,*) x, Qext, Qabs
        end if
        if(ier.eq.1) then
          write(7,*) 'rrrrrrrrrrrrrrrr'
          write(*,*) 'rrrrrrrrrrrrrrrr'
        end if
        if(ier.eq.2) then
          pause
          stop
        end if
      end do
c*
      write (7,5)
      close (7)
      stop
      end
c------------------------------------------------------------
c **********   shexqnn - Spheres: homogeneous
c                        Theory: exact
c                        Results: efficiency factors
c------------------------------------------------------------
      subroutine shexqnn(ri, x, Qext, Qsca, Qabs, Qbk,
     *                   Qpr, albedo, g, ier)
```

```
      parameter(nterms=630000)
      implicit real*8(a-h,o-q,t-z), complex*16(r-s)
      dimension ru(2*nterms)
      dimension fact(0:1)
      data factor / 1d250 /
      data eps    / 1d-15 /
      data fact / 1d0, 1d250 /
c* efficiency factors
      ier  = 0
      Qext = 0d0
      Qsca = 0d0
      Qabs = 0d0
      Qbk  = 0d0
      Qpr  = 0d0
      albedo = 0d0
      g      = 0d0
c* null argument
      if(x.le.1d-6) then
       ier=1
       return
      end if
c*
      pi = 4d0 * datan(1d0)
      ax = 1d0 / x
      b = 2d0 * ax**2
      ss = (0d0,0d0)
      s3 = (0d0,-1d0)
      an = 3d0
c* choice of number for subroutine aa [Loskutov (1971)]
      y = cdsqrt(ri*dconjg(ri))*x
      num = 1.25 * y + 15.5
      if(y.lt.1d0) go to 11
      if(y.gt.100d0.and.y.lt.50000d0) go to 12
      if(y.ge.50000d0) go to 13
      go to 14
   11 num = 7.5 * y + 9.0
      go to 14
   12 num = 1.0625 * y + 28.5
```

```
      go to 14
13    num=1.005*y+50.5
14    continue
      if(num.gt.2*nterms) then
        ier = 2
        write(*,*) '2*nterms, num=', 2*nterms, num
        return
      end if
c* logarithmic derivative to Bessel function
c* (complex argument)
      call aa(ax,ri,num,ru)
c* Bessel functions (first terms)
      ass = dsqrt(pi / 2d0 * ax)
      w1 =  2d0 / pi * ax
        Si = dsin(x)/x
        Co = dcos(x)/x
c n=0
        besJ0 = Si / ass
        besY0 = - Co / ass
        iu0 = 0
c n=1
        besJ1 = (Si * ax - Co) / ass
        besY1 = (- Co * ax - Si) / ass
        iu1 = 0
        iu2 = 0
c* Mie coefficients (first term)
      s = ru(1) / ri + ax
      s1 = s * besJ1 - besJ0
      s2 = s * besY1 - besY0
      ra0 = s1 / (s1 - s3 * s2)
      s = ru(1) * ri + ax
      s1 = s * besJ1 - besJ0
      s2 = s * besY1 - besY0
      rb0 = s1 / (s1 - s3 * s2)
c* efficiency factors (first term)
      r = -1.5d0*(ra0-rb0)
      Qext = an * (ra0 + rb0)
      Qsca = an * (ra0 * dconjg(ra0) + rb0 *
```

```
      *           dconjg(rb0))
c*
      z = -1d0
      do i = 2, 100 000 000
          an = an + 2d0
          an2 = an - 2d0
c* Bessel functions
          if(iu1.eq.iu0) then
              besY2 = an2 * ax * besY1 - besY0
          else
              besY2 = an2 * ax * besY1 - besY0 / factor
          end if
          if(dabs(besY2).gt.1d300) then
            besY2 = besY2 / factor
            iu2 = iu1 + 1
          end if
          besJ2 = (w1 + besY2 * besJ1) / besY1
c* Mie coefficients
      s = ru(i) / ri + i * ax
      s1 = s * besJ2 / fact(iu2) - besJ1 / fact(iu1)
      s2 = s * besY2 * fact(iu2) - besY1 * fact(iu1)
      ra1 = s1 / (s1 - s3 * s2)
c
      s = ru(i) * ri + i * ax
      s1 = s * besJ2 / fact(iu2) - besJ1 / fact(iu1)
      s2 = s * besY2 * fact(iu2) - besY1 * fact(iu1)
      rb1 = s1 / (s1 - s3 * s2)
c* efficiency factors
      z = -z
      rr = z * (i + 0.5d0) * (ra1 - rb1)
      r = r + rr
      ss = ss + (i - 1d0) * (i + 1d0) / i *
      *     (ra0 * dconjg(ra1) + rb0 * dconjg(rb1)) +
      *     an2 / i / (i - 1d0) * (ra0 * dconjg(rb0))
      qq = an * (ra1 + rb1)
      Qext = Qext + qq
      Qsca = Qsca + an * (ra1 * dconjg(ra1) +
      *       rb1 * dconjg(rb1))
```

```
      if(dabs(qq / qext).lt.eps) go to 1
c* Bessel functions
        besJ0 = besJ1
        besJ1 = besJ2
        besY0 = besY1
        besY1 = besY2
          iu0 =   iu1
          iu1 =   iu2
          ra0 =   ra1
          rb0 =   rb1
      end do
c* end of cycle
   1  continue
c* efficiency factors (final calculations)
      Qext = b * Qext
      Qsca = b * Qsca
      Qbk = 2d0 * b * r * dconjg(r)
      Qpr = Qext - 2d0 * b * ss
      Qabs = Qext - Qsca
      albedo = Qsca / Qext
      g = (Qext - Qpr) / Qsca
      return
      end
c------------------------------------------------------------
c aa-subroutine for calculations of the ratio of
c    derivative to the function for Bessel functions
c    of half order with complex argument: J'(n)/J(n).
c    The calculations are given by the recursive
c    expression ''from top to bottom'' beginning
c    from n=num.
c    ru-array of results.
c    a=1/x (a=2*pi*a(particle radius)/lambda -
c    size parameter).
c    ri - complex refractive index.
c August 1989, AO LGU
c------------------------------------------------------------
      subroutine aa(a, ri, num, ru)
      implicit real*8 (a-h,o-q,t-z), complex*16 (r-s)
```

```
dimension ru(num)
s=  a / ri
ru(num) = (num + 1d0) * s
num1 = num - 1
do j = 1, num1
  i = num - j
  i1 = i + 1
  s1 = i1 * s
  ru(i) = s1 - 1d0 / (ru(i1) + s1)
end do
return
end
```

```
c*NVVMIE.dat ******************************************
1.6              0.1                  ri: refractive index
100000.                               x: x1
100000.                               x: dx
500000.                               x: x2
```

ACKNOWLEDGEMENTS

I am indepted to J. Dorschner, D. Dubkova, Th. Henning, E. Kasimova, A. Perelman and D. Semenov for helpful comments and suggestions. I appreciate the discussions of light scattering by non-spherical particles with Victor Farafonov and Bernhard Michel. My special thanks to Vladimir Il'in for permanent consultations and careful reading of manuscript. This research was partly supported by the INTAS grant (Open Call 99/652) and by grant 1088.2003.2 of the President of the Russian Federation for leading scientific schools.

Table 13 Efficiency factors, albedo and asymmetry parameter as calculated by the program NVVMIE.

x	Q_{ext}	Q_{sca}	Q_{abs}	Q_{bk}	Q_{pr}	Λ	g
			$m = 1.6 + 0.0i$				
100 000.00	2.001065	2.001065	0.000000	2454.059	0.39732	1.00000	0.80144
200 000.00	2.000489	2.000489	0.000000	4668.846	0.39678	1.00000	0.80166
300 000.00	2.000470	2.000470	0.000000	7268.697	0.39694	1.00000	0.80158
500 000.00	2.000292	2.000292	0.000000	12028.586	0.39682	1.00000	0.80162
1 000 000.00	2.000243	2.000243	0.000000	23259.068	0.39714	1.00000	0.80146
2 000 000.00	2.000145	2.000145	0.000000	47309.539	0.39682	1.00000	0.80161
3 000 000.00	2.000122	2.000122	0.000000	71158.654	0.39710	1.00000	0.80146
5 000 000.00	2.000092	2.000092	0.000000	114254.746	0.39710	1.00000	0.80146
6 283 185.31	2.000073	2.000073	0.000000	144270.285	0.39689	1.00000	0.80156
Geometrical optics	2.000000				0.39695		0.80153
			$m = 1.6 + 0.1i$				
100 000.00	2.000924	1.108838	0.892086	0.054653	0.96002	0.55416	0.93873
200 000.00	2.000582	1.108537	0.892046	0.054653	0.95998	0.55411	0.93872
300 000.00	2.000444	1.108412	0.892032	0.054653	0.95997	0.55408	0.93871
500 000.00	2.000316	1.108295	0.892021	0.054653	0.95996	0.55406	0.93870
1 000 000.00	2.000199	1.108187	0.892012	0.054653	0.95995	0.55404	0.93870
2 000 000.00	2.000125	1.108117	0.892008	0.054653	0.95994	0.55402	0.93869
3 000 000.00	2.000096	1.108089	0.892007	0.054653	0.95994	0.55402	0.93869
5 000 000.00	2.000068	1.108063	0.892006	0.054653	0.95994	0.55401	0.93869
6 283 185.31	2.000059	1.108053	0.892005	0.054653	0.95993	0.55401	0.93869
Geometrical optics	2.000000		0.89199	0.054653	0.95993	0.55401	0.93869

REFERENCES

Aannestad, P.A. (1995) *Astrophys. J.*, **443**, 653

Aannestad, P.A. and Greenberg, J.M. (1983) *Astrophys. J.*, **272**, 551

Aden, A.L. and Kerker, M. (1951) *J. Appl. Phys.*, **22**, 1242

Aguirre, A. (1999) *Astrophys. J.*, **512**, L19

Alibés, A., Labay, J. and Canal, R. (2001) *Astron. Astrophys.*, **370**, 1103

Anders, E. and Grevesse, N. (1989) *Geochim. Cosmochim. Acta*, **53**, 197

Andersen, A.C., Sotelo, J.A., Pustovit, V.N. and Niklasson, G.A. (2002) *Astron. Astrophys.*, **386**, 296 [Erratum: (2003) **411**, 481]

Andersen, A.C., Sotelo, J.A., Niklasson, G.A. and Pustovit, V.N. (2003) *astro-ph*/0310343

André, M.K., Oliveira, C.M., Howk, J.C., Ferlet, R., Désert, J.-M., Hébrard, G., Lacour, S., Lecavelier des Étangs, A., Vidal-Madjar, A. and Moos, H.W. (2003) *Astrophys. J.*, **591**, 1000

Arce, H.G. and Goodman, A.A. (1999) *Astrophys. J.*, **512**, L135

Arce, H.G., Goodman, A.A., Bastien, P., Manset, N. and Sumner, M. (1998) *Astrophys. J.*, **499**, L93

Arendt, R.G., Odegard, N., Weiland, J.L., Sodroski, T.J., Hauser, M.G., Dwek, E., Kelsall, T., Moseley, S.H., Silverberg, R.F., Leisawitz, D., Mitchell, K., Reach, W.T. and Wright, E.L. (1998) *Astrophys. J.*, **508**, 74

Asano, S. (1979) *Appl. Optics*, **18**, 712

Asano, S. and Sato, M. (1980) *Appl. Optics*, **19**, 962

Asano, S. and Yamamoto, G. (1975) *Appl. Optics*, **14**, 29

Aspnes, D.E (1982) *Thin Solid Films*, **89**, 249

Babenko, V.A., Astafyeva, L.G. and Kuz'min, V.N. (2003) *Electromagnetic scattering in disperse media: inhomogeneous and anisotropic particles*, Springer-Praxis

Barabas, M. (1987) *J. Opt. Soc. America*, **A4**, 2240

Barber, P.W. and Hill, S.C. (1990) *Light Scattering by Particles: Computational Methods*, World Scientific, Singapore

Barber, P.W. and Yeh, C. (1975) *Appl. Optics*, **14**, 2864

Bastien, P. and Ménard, F. (1988) *Astrophys. J.*, **326**, 334

Bayvel, L.P. and Jones, A.R. (1981) *Electromagnetic Scattering and Its Applications*, Appl. Sci. Publ., London

Birchak, J.R., Gardner, L.G., Hipp, J.W. and Victor, J.M. (1974) *Proc. IEEE*, **62**, 93

Bohren, C.F. and Huffman, D.R. (1983) *Absorption and Scattering of Light by Small Particles*, John Wiley and Sons, New York

Bosma, P.B. (1993a) *Astron. Astrophys.*, **276**, 303

Bosma, P.B. (1993b) *Astron. Astrophys.*, **279**, 572

Böttcher, C.J.F. (1952) *Theory of Electric Polarization*, Elsevier, Amsterdam

Bowyer, S., Drake, J.J. and Vennes, S. (2000) *Annu. Rev. Astron. Astrophys.*, **38**, 231

Bruggeman, D.A.G. (1935) *Ann. Phys.*, **24**, 636

Burnashev, V.I. (1999) *Crimean Observ. Bull.*, **95**, 91
Cahalan, R.F. (2000) In *IRS 2000: Current Problems in Atmospheric Radiation*, Abstracts, p. 61
Cambrésy, L., Boulanger, F., Lagache, G. and Stepnik, B. (2001) *Astron. Astrophys.*, **375**, 999
Cardelli, J.A. and Savage, B.D. (1989) *Astrophys. J.*, **325**, 864
Cardelli, J.A., Clayton, G.C. and Mathis, J.S. (1989) *Astrophys. J.*, **345**, 245
Chhowalla, M., Wang, H., Sano, N., Teo, K.B.K., Lee, S.B. and Amaratunga, G.A.J. (2003) *Phys. Rev. Lett.*, **90**, 155504
Chini, R., Krügel, E. and Kreysa, E. (1986) *Astron. Astrophys.*, **167**, 315
Chlewicki, G. and Greenberg, J.M. (1990) *Astrophys. J.*, **365**, 230
Chýlek, P. and Videen, G. (1998) *Optics Comm.*, **146**, 15
Chýlek, P., Videen, G., Geldart, D.J.W., Dobbie, J.S. and Tso, H.C.W. (2000) In *Light Scattering by Nonspherical Particles*, ed. by M.I. Mishchenko *et al.*, Academic Press, San Francisco, p. 274
Clayton, G.C. and Cardelli, J.A. (1988) *Astron. J.*, **96**, 695
Clayton, G.C., Gordon, K.D., Salama, F., Allamandola, L.J., Martin, P.G., Snow, T.P., Whittet, D.C.B., Witt, A.N. and Wolff, M.J. (2003a) *Astrophys. J.*, **592**, 947
Clayton, G.C., Wolff, M.J., Sofia, U.J., Gordon, K.D. and Misselt, K.A. (2003b) *Astrophys. J.*, **588**, 871
Code, A.D. and Whitney, B.A. (1995) *Astrophys. J.*, **441**, 440
Collinge, M.J. and Draine, B.T. (2003) *astro-ph/03111304*
Collison, A.J. and Fix, J.D. (1991) *Astrophys. J.*, **368**, 545
Daniel, J.-Y. (1980) *Astron. Astrophys.*, **87**, 204
Davies, L. and Greenstein, J.L. (1951) *Astrophys. J.*, **114**, 206
Debye, P. (1909) *Ann. Phys.*, **30**, 57
d'Hendecourt, L., Joblin, C. and Jones A. (1999) (ed.) *Solid Interstellar Matter: the ISO Revolution* Springer-Verlag, Berlin
Dolginov, A.Z., Gnedin, Yu.N. and Silant'ev, N.A. (1979) *Propagation and Polarization of Radiation in Cosmic Medium*, Nauka, Moscow
Dombrovskii, V.A. (1949) *Doklady Akad. Nauk Armenia*, **10**, 199
Dorschner, J. (1973) *Astrophys. Space Sci.*, **25**, 405
Dorschner, J. (2003) In *Astromineralogy*, ed. by Th. Henning, Springer, p. 1
Dorschner, J. and Henning, Th. (1995) *Astron. Astrophys. Rev.*, **6**, 271
Dorschner, J., Begemann, B., Henning, Th., Jäger, C. and Mutschke, H. (1995) *Astron. Astrophys.*, **300**, 503
Draine, B.T. (1984) *Astrophys. J.*, **277**, L71
Draine, B.T. (1985) *Astrophys. J. Suppl.*, **57**, 587
Draine, B.T. (2000) In *Light Scattering by Nonspherical Particles*, ed. by M.I. Mishchenko *et al.*, Academic Press, San Francisco, p. 131
Draine, B.T. (2003a) *Annu. Rev. Astron. Astrophys.*, **41**, 241
Draine, B.T. (2003b) In *The Cold Universe*, ed. by D. Pfenniger, Springer, in press (*astro-ph/0304488*)
Draine, B.T. and Lazarian, A. (1999) *Astrophys. J.*, **512**, 740

Draine, B.T. and Lee, H.M. (1984) *Astrophys. J.*, **285**, 89 [Erratum: (1987) **318**, 485]
Draine, B.T. and Malhotra, S. (1994) *Astrophys. J.*, **414**, 632
Draine, B.T. and Weingartner, J.C. (1996) *Astrophys. J.*, **470**, 551
Draine, B.T. and Weingartner, J.C. (1997) *Astrophys. J.*, **480**, 633
Drimmel, R., Cabrera-Lavers, A. and López-Corredoira, M. (2003) *Astron. Astrophys.*, **409**, 205
Dubkova, D.N. (2001) *Diploma Thesis*, St. Petersburg University
Duley, W.W. and Seahra, S. (1998) *Astrophys. J.*, **507**, 874
Dullemond, C.P. and Turolla, R. (2000) *Astron. Astrophys.*, **360**, 1187
Dunne, L., Eales, S., Ivison, R., Morgan, H. and Edmunds, M. (2003) *Nature*, **424**, 285
Dutra, C.M. and Bica, E. (2002) *Astron. Astrophys.*, **383**, 631
Dutra, C.M., Ahumada, A.V., Clariá, J.J., Bica, E. and Barbuy, B. (2003a) *Astron. Astrophys.*, **408**, 287
Dutra, C.M., Santiago, B.X., Bica, E. and Barbuy, B. (2003b) *Monthly Notices RAS*, **338**, 253
Dwek, E. (2004) *astro-ph/0401074*
Efstathiou, A. and Rowan-Robinson, M. (1990) *Monthly Notices RAS*, **245**, 275
Egan, M.P., Spagna, G.F. and Leung, C.M. (1988) *Computer Physics Comm.*, **48**, 271
Ehrenfreund, P. (1999) In *Solid Interstellar Matter: the ISO Revolution*, ed. by L. d'Hendecourt, C. Joblin and A. Jones, Springer-Verlag, Berlin, p. 231
Farafonov, V.G. (1983) *Differential Equations (Sov.)*, **19**, 1765
Farafonov, V.G. (1994a) *Optics Spectrosc.*, **76**, 79
Farafonov, V.G. (1994b) *Optics Spectrosc.*, **77**, 455
Farafonov, V.G. (2000) *Optics Spectrosc.*, **88**, 492
Farafonov, V.G. (2001) *Optics Spectrosc.*, **90**, 743
Farafonov, V.G. and Il'in V.B. (2001) *Optics Spectrosc.*, **91**, 960
Farafonov, V.G., Il'in V.B. and Henning, T. (1999) *J. Quant. Spectrosc. Rad. Transfer*, **63**, 205
Farafonov, V.G., Il'in V.B. and Prokop'eva, M.S. (2002) *Optics Spectrosc.*, **92**, 567
Farafonov, V.G., Il'in, V.B. and Prokop'eva, M.S. (2003) *J. Quant. Spectrosc. Rad. Transfer*, **79–80**, 599
Farafonov, V.G., Voshchinnikov, N.V. and Somsikov, V.V. (1996) *Appl. Optics*, **35**, 5412
Fischer, O. (1993) *PhD Thesis*, Friedrich-Schiller-Universität, Jena
Fitzpatrick, E.L. (1997) *Astrophys. J.*, **482**, L199
Fitzpatrick, E.L. (1999) *Publ. Astron. Soc. Pacific*, **111**, 163
Fitzpatrick, E.L. (2004) *astro-ph/0401344*
Fitzpatrick, E.L. and Massa, D.L. (1986) *Astrophys. J.*, **307**, 286
Fitzpatrick, E.L. and Massa, D.L. (1990) *Astrophys. J. Suppl.*, **72**, 163
Fogel, M.E. and Leung, C.M. (1998) *Astrophys. J.*, **501**, 175

Fosalba, P., Lazarian, A., Prunet, S. and Tauber, J.A. (2002a) In
  Astrophysical Polarized Backgrounds, ed. by S. Cecchini *et al.*, AIP
  Conf. Proc., **609**, p. 44
Fosalba, P., Lazarian, A., Prunet, S. and Tauber, J.A. (2002b) *Astrophys.
  J.*, **564**, 762
Friedemann, C. and Gürtler, J. (1986) *Astrophys. Space Sci.*, **128**, 71
Frisch, P.C., Dorschner, J.M., Geiss, J., Greenberg, J.M., Grün, E.,
  Landgraf, M., Hoppe, P., Jones, A.P., Krätschmer, W., Linde, T.J.,
  Morfill, G.E., Reach, W., Slavin, J.D., Svestka, J., Witt, A.N. and
  Zank, G.P. (1999) *Astrophys. J.*, **525**, 492
Garnett, J.C.M. (1904) *Phil. Trans. R. Soc.*, **A 203**, 385
Geist, J. (1998) In *Handbook of Optical Constants of Solids III*, ed. by
  E.D. Palik, Academic Press, New York, p. 519
Gojian, V., Wright, E.L. and Chary, R.R. (2000) *Astrophys. J.*, **536**, 550
Gold, T. (1952) *Monthly Notices RAS*, **112**, 215
Gonçalves, J., Galli, D. and Walmsley, M. (2003) *astro-ph*/0311171
Goodman, A.A., Jones, T.T., Lada, E.A. and Myers, P.C. (1995)
  Astrophys. J., **448**, 748
Gordon, K.D., Misselt, K.A., Witt, A.N. and Clayton, G.C. (2001)
  Astrophys. J., **551**, 269
Greenberg, J.M. (1968) *Interstellar Grains*, In *Stars and Stellar Systems*,
  Vol. VII, ed. by B.M. Middlehurst and L. H. Aller, Univ. Chicago
  Press, p. 221
Greenberg, J.M. (1978) *Interstellar Dust*, In *Cosmic Dust*, ed. by J.A.M.
  McDonnel, p. 187
Greenberg, J.M. and Chlewicki, G. (1987) *Quart. J. RAS*, **28**, 312
Greenberg, J.M. and Li, A. (1996a) In *The Cosmic Dust Connection*, ed.
  by J.M. Greenberg, Kluwer, p. 43
Greenberg, J.M. and Li, A. (1996b) *Astron. Astrophys.*, **309**, 258
Greenberg, J.M. and Meltzer, A.S. (1960) *Astrophys. J.*, **132**, 667
Greenberg, J.M. and Shah, G.A. (1966) *Astrophys. J.*, **145**, 63
Greenberg, J.M., Pedersen, N.E. and Pedersen, J.C. (1961) *J. Appl.
  Phys.*, **32**, 233
Groenewegen, M.A.T. (1993) *PhD Thesis*, University of Amsterdam
Grün, E. (1997) *Astron. Astrophys.*, **317**, 503
Gurwich, I., Kleiman, M., Shiloah, N. and Cohen, A. (2000) *Appl. Optics*,
  39, 470
Gurwich, I., Shiloah, N. and Kleiman, M. (1999) *J. Quant. Spectrosc.
  Rad. Transfer*, **63**, 217
Gurwich, I., Kleiman, M., Shiloah, N. and Oaknin, D. (2003) *J. Quant.
  Spectrosc. Rad. Transfer*, **79–80**, 649
Gustafson, B.Å.S. (1996) *J. Quant. Spectrosc. Rad. Transfer*, **55**, 663
Gustafson, B.Å.S. (2000) In *Light Scattering by Nonspherical Particles*,
  ed. by M.I. Mishchenko *et al.*, Academic Press, San Francisco, p. 367
Gustafson, B.Å.S., Greenberg, J.M., Kolokolova, L., Xu, Y.-l. and
  Stognienko, R. (2001) In *Interplanetary Dust*, ed. by E. Grün *et al.*,
  Berlin, Springer, p. 509

Gürtler, J., Schielicke, R., Dorschner, J. and Friedemann, C. (1982) *Astron. Nachr.*, **303**, 105

Güttler, A. (1952) *Ann. Phys.*, **6**, Bd. 11, 65

Hadamcik, E., Renard, J.B., Levasseur-Regourd, A.C. and Worms, J.C. (2003) *J. Quant. Spectrosc. Rad. Transfer*, **79–80**, 679

Hage, J.I. and Greenberg, J.M. (1990) *Astrophys. J.*, **361**, 251

Hakkila, J., Myers, J.M., Stidham, B.J. and Hartmann, D.H. (1997) *Astron. J.*, **114**, 2043

Hall, J.S. (1949) *Science*, **109**, 166

Hashin, Z. and Shtrikman, S. (1962) *J. Appl. Phys.*, **33**, 3125

Hegmann, M. and Kegel, W.H. (2003) *Monthly Notices RAS*, **342**, 453

Heiles, C. (1996) *Astrophys. J.*, **462**, 316

Heiles, C. (1997) *Astrophys. J. Suppl.*, **111**, 245

Heiles, C. (2000) *Astron. J.*, **119**, 923

Henning, Th. (1999) In *Solid Interstellar Matter: the ISO Revolution*, ed. by L. d'Hendecourt, C. Joblin and A. Jones, Springer-Verlag, Berlin, p. 247

Henning, Th. (2001) In *The Formation of Binary Stars*, ed. by B. Mathieu and H. Zinnecker, IAU Symp., **200**, p. 567

Henning, Th. (ed.) (2003a) *Astromineralogy*, Springer

Henning, Th. (2003b) In *Astromineralogy*, ed. by Th. Henning, Springer, p. 266

Henning, Th. and Mutschke, H. (2000) In *Thermal Emission Spectroscopy and Analysis of Dust, Disks and Regolits*, ed. by M.L. Sitko *et al.*, ASP Conf. Ser., **196**, p. 253

Henning, Th., Begemann, B., Mutschke, H. and Dorschner, J. (1995) *Astron. Astrophys. Suppl.*, **112**, 143

Henning, Th., Il'in, V.B., Krivova, N.A., Michel, B. and Voshchinnikov, N.V. (1999) *Astron. Astrophys. Suppl.*, **136**, 405

Henyey, L.G. and Greenstein, J.K. (1941) *Astrophys. J.*, **93**, 70

Hiltner, W.A. (1949) *Science*, **109**, 165

Höfflich, P. (1991) *Astron. Astrophys.*, **246**, 481

Hong, S.S. and Greenberg, J.M. (1980) *Astron. Astrophys.*, **88**, 194

Hovenier, J.W. (1994) *Appl. Optics*, **33**, 8318

Hovenier, J.W. (ed) (1996) *J. Quant. Spectrosc. Rad. Transfer*, **55**, N 5

Hovenier, J.W. (2000) In *Light Scattering by Nonspherical Particles*, ed. by M.I. Mishchenko *et al.*, Academic Press, San Francisco, p. 355

Hovenier, J.W., Lumme, K., Mishchenko, M.I., Voshchinnikov, N.V., Mackowski, D.W. and Rahola, J. (1996) *J. Quant. Spectrosc. Rad. Transfer*, **55**, 695

Hovenier, J.W., Volten, H., Muñoz, O., van der Zande, W.J. and Waters, L.B.F.M. (2003) *J. Quant. Spectrosc. Rad. Transfer*, **79–80**, 741

Hoyle, F. and Wickramasinghe, N.C. (1962) *Monthly Notices RAS*, **124**, 417

Hummer, D.G. and Rybicki, G.B. (1971) *Monthly Notices RAS*, **152**, 1

Iatì, M.A., Cecchi-Pestellini, C., Williams, D.A., Borghese, F., Denti, P., Saija, R. and Aiello, S. (2001) *Monthly Notices RAS*, **322**, 749

Il'in, A.E. (1987) *Astrofisika*, **27**, 477
Il'in, V.B. and Henning, Th. (2003) *Astron. Astrophys.*, in preparation
Il'in, V.B., Loskutov, A.A. and Farafonov, V.G. (2004) *Comput. Mathem. Mathem. Phys.*, **44**, 349
Il'in, V.B., Prokop'eva, M.S. and Henning, Th. (2003) *Astron. Astrophys.*, in preparation
Il'in, V.B., Voshchinnikov N.V., Farafonov V.G., Henning, Th. and Perelman A.Ya. (2002) In *Optics of Cosmic Dust*, ed. by G. Videen and M. Kocifaj M., Kluwer, p. 71
Il'in, V.B., Voshchinnikov N.V., Babenko, V.A., Beletsky, S.A., Henning, Th., Jäger, C., Khlebtsov, N.G., Litvinov, P.V., Mutschke, H., Tishkovets, V.P. and Waters, R. (2003) *astro-ph/0308175*
Iskander, M.F. and Lakhtakia, A. (1984) *Appl. Optics*, **23**, 948
Isobe, S. (1973) *Publ. Astron. Soc. Japan*, **25**, 101
Ivezić, Ž. and Elitzur, M. (1997) *Monthly Notices RAS*, **287**, 799
Ivezić, Ž., Groenewegen, M.A.T., Men'shchikov, A.B. and Szczerba, R. (1997) *Monthly Notices RAS*, **291**, 121
Jäger, C., Il'in, V.B., Henning, Th., Mutschke, H., Fabian, D., Semenov, D.A. and Voshchinnikov, N.V. (2003) *J. Quant. Spectrosc. Radiat. Transfer*, **79–80**, 765
Jenniskens, P. and Greenberg, J.M. (1993) *Astron. Astrophys.*, **274**, 439
Johnson, H.L. (1968) *Interstellar Extinction*, In *Stars and Stellar Systems*, Vol. VII, ed. by B.M. Middlehurst and L. H. Aller, Univ. Chicago Press, p. 167
Joiner, D.A. and Leung, C.M. (2003) *Astrophys. J.*, **593**, 402
Jones, A.P. (1988) *Monthly Notices RAS*, **234**, 209
Jones, A.P. (2000) *J. Geophys. Res.*, **105**, 10257
Jones, A.R. (1999) *Progr. Energy Combust. Sci.*, **25**, 1
Jones, R.V. and Spitzer, L. (1967) *Astrophys. J.*, **147**, 943
Juett, A.M., Schulz, N.S. and Chakrabarty, D. (2003) *astro-ph/0312205*
Juvela, M. and Padoan, P. (2003) *Astron. Astrophys.*, **397**, 201
Kahnert, F.M. (2003) *J. Quant. Spectrosc. Radiat. Transfer*, **79–80**, 775
Kärkkäinen, K., Sihvola, A., Nikoskinen, K. and Pekonen, O. (1999) *Electromagnetic Laboratory, Helsinki University of Technology*, Report **291**
Kemp, J.C. and Wolstencroft, R.D. (1972) *Astrophys. J.*, **176**, L115
Khotygin, A.F., Il'in, V.B. and Voshchinnikov, N.V. (1997) *Astron. Astrophys.*, **323**, 189
Kim, S.-H. and Martin, P.G. (1994) *Astrophys. J.*, **431**, 783
Kim, S.-H. and Martin, P.G. (1995) *Astrophys. J.*, **444**, 293
Kim, S.-H., Martin, P.G. and Hendry, P.D. (1994) *Astrophys. J.*, **422**, 164
Knude, J. and Høg, E. (1999) *Astron. Astrophys.*, **341**, 451
Kokhanovsky, A. (1999) *Optics of Light Scattering Media: Problems and Solutions*, John Wiley, Chichester
Kolokolova, L. and Gustafson, B.Å.S. (2001) *J. Quant. Spectrosc. Rad. Transfer*, **70**, 611

Kolokolova, L., Gustafson, B.Å.S., Mishchenko, M.I. and Videen, G. (ed.) (2003) *J. Quant. Spectrosc. Rad. Transfer*, **79**–**80**

Kreibig, U. and Vollmer, M. (1995) *Optical Properties of Metal Clusters*, Springer, Berlin

Krügel, E. (2003) *The Physics of Interstellar Dust*, Institute of Physics Publishing, Bristol

Ku, J.C. and Felske, J.D. (1984) *J. Quant. Spectrosc. Rad. Transfer*, **31**, 569

Lakhtakia, A. and Durney, C.H. (1983) *IEEE Trans. MTT*, **31**, 640

Laor, A. and Draine, B.T. (1993) *Astrophys. J.*, **402**, 441

Larson, K.A., Wolff, M.J., Roberge, W.G., Whittet, D.C.B. and He, L. (2000) *Astrophys. J.*, **532**, 1021

Lazarian, A. (1995) *Astrophys. J.*, **451**, 660

Lazarian, A. (2000) In *Cosmic Evolution and Galaxy Formation: Structure, Interactions, and Feedback*, ed. by J. Franco *et al.*, ASP Conf. Ser., **215**, p. 69

Lazarian, A. (2003) *J. Quant. Spectrosc. Rad. Transfer*, **79**–**80**, 881

Lazarian, A., Goodman, A.A. and Myers, P.C. (1997) *Astrophys. J.*, **490**, 273

Lefèvre, J., Bergeat, J. and Daniel, J.-Y. (1982) *Astron. Astrophys.*, **114**, 346

Lefèvre, J., Bergeat, J. and Daniel, J.-Y. (1983) *Astron. Astrophys.*, **121**, 51

Leksina, I.E. and Penkina, N.V. (1967) *Fizika metallov i metalloved.*, **23**, 344

Leung, C.M. (1976) *J. Quant. Spectrosc. Rad. Transfer*, **16**, 559

Li, A. and Draine, B.T. (2001) *Astrophys. J.*, **551**, 807

Li, A. and Greenberg, J.M. (1997) *Astron. Astrophys.*, **323**, 566

Li, A. and Greenberg, J.M. (1998) *Astron. Astrophys.*, **339**, 591

Lind, A.C. and Greenberg, J.M. (1966) *J. Appl. Phys.*, **37**, 3195

Lindblad, B. (1935) *Nature*, **135**, 133

Lodders, K. (2003) *Astrophys. J.*, **591**, 1220

Looyenga, H. (1965) *Physica*, **31**, 401

Lopez, B., Mékarnia, D. and Lefèvre, J. (1995) *Astron. Astrophys.*, **296**, 752

Loskutov, V.M. (1971) *Trudy Astron. Obs. Leningrad Univ.*, **28**, 14

Lucas, P.W. (2003) *J. Quant. Spectrosc. Rad. Transfer*, **79**–**80**, 921

Lumme, K. (ed.) (1998) *J. Quant. Spectrosc. Rad. Transfer*, **60**, N 3

Lumme, K. and Rahola, J. (1994) *Astrophys. J.*, **425**, 563

Mann, I. (1998) *Earth Planets Space*, **50**, 465

Martin, P.G. (1972) *Monthly Notices RAS*, **159**, 179

Martin, P.G. (1974) *Astrophys. J.*, **187**, 461

Martin, P.G. (1975) *Astrophys. J.*, **202**, 389

Martin, P.G. (1978) *Cosmic Dust*, Oxford Univ. Press, Oxford

Martin, P.G. and Angel, J.P.R. (1976) *Astrophys. J.*, **207**, 126

Martin, P.G. and Campbell, B. (1976) *Astrophys. J.*, **208**, 727

Martin, P.G. and Whittet, D.C.B. (1990) *Astrophys. J.*, **357**, 113

Martin, P.G., Adamson, A.J., Whittet, D.C.B., Hough, J.H., Bailey, J.A., Kim, S.-H., Sato, S., Tamura, M. and Yamashita, T. (1992) *Astrophys. J.*, **392**, 691

Martin, P.G., Clayton, G.C. and Wolff, M.J. (1999) *Astrophys. J.*, **510**, 905

Martin, P.G., Illing, R., and Angel, J.R.P. (1972) *Monthly Notices RAS*, **159**, 191

Mathis, J.S. (1979) *Astrophys. J.*, **232**, 747

Mathis, J.S. (1986) *Astrophys. J.*, **308**, 281

Mathis, J.S. (1994) *Astrophys. J.*, **422**, 176

Mathis, J.S. (1996) *Astrophys. J.*, **472**, 643

Mathis, J.S. and Whiffen, G. (1989) *Astrophys. J.*, **341**, 808

Mathis, J.S., Rumpl, W. and Nordsieck, K.H. (1977) *Astrophys. J.*, **217**, 425

Matsumura, M. and Seki, M. (1996) *Astrophys. J.*, **456**, 557

Mennella, V., Colangeli, L., Bussoletti, E., Palumbo, P. and Rotundi, A. (1998) *Astrophys. J.*, **507**, L177

Men'shchikov, A.B. and Henning, Th. (1997) *Astron. Astrophys.*, **318**, 879

Men'shchikov, A.B., Henning, Th. and Fischer, O. (1999) *Astrophys. J.*, **519**, 257

Men'shchikov, A.B., Balega, Yu., Blöcker, Th., Osterbart, R. and Weigelt, G. (2001) *Astron. Astrophys.*, **368**, 497

Meyer, D.M., Jura, M. and Cardelli, J.A. (1998) *Astrophys. J.*, **493**, 222

Mie, G. (1908) *Ann. Phys.*, **25**, 377

Milton, G.W. (1980) *Appl. Phys. Lett.*, **37**, 300

Mishchenko, M.I. and Travis, L.D. (1994a) *Appl. Optics*, **33**, 7206

Mishchenko, M.I. and Travis, L.D. (1994b) *Optics Comm.*, **109**, 16

Mishchenko, M.I., Hovenier, J. and Travis, L.D. (ed.) (2000a) *Light Scattering by Nonspherical Particles*, Academic Press, San Francisco

Mishchenko, M.I., Travis, L.D. and Hovenier, J. (ed.) (1999) *J. Quant. Spectrosc. Rad. Transfer*, **63**, N 2-6

Mishchenko, M.I. Travis, L.D. and Lacis, A.A. (2002) *Scattering, Absorption, and Emission of Light by Small Particles*, Cambridge Univ. Press

Mishchenko, M.I., Travis, L.D. and Mackowski, D.W. (1996) *J. Quant. Spectrosc. Radiat. Transfer*, **55**, 535

Mishchenko, M.I., Wiscombe, W.J., Hovenier, J. and Travis, L.D. (2000b) In *Light Scattering by Nonspherical Particles*, ed. by M.I. Mishchenko et al., Academic Press, San Francisco, p. 30

Misselt, K.A., Gordon, K.D., Clayton, G.C. and Wolff, M.J. (2001) *Astrophys. J.*, **551**, 277

Molster, F.J. (2000) *PhD Thesis*, University of Amsterdam

Moreno, F., Muñoz, O., Lópes-Moreno, J.J., Molina, A., and Ortitz, J.L. (2002) *Icarus*, **156**, 474

Morgan, H.L., Dunne, L., Eales, S.A., Ivison, R.J., and Edmunds, M.G. (2003) *Astrophys. J.*, **597**, L33

Morrison, R. and McCammon, D. (1983) *Astrophys. J.*, **270**, 119

Muinonen, K. (2002) In *Electromagnetic and Light Scattering by Nonspherical Particle*, ed. by B.Å.S. Gustafson, L. Kolokolova and G. Videen, Army Res. Lab., Adelphi, p. 219

Nandy, K. (1966) *Publ. Roy. Obs. Edinburgh*, **5**, 233

Niccolini, G., Woitke, P. and Lopez, B. (2003) *Astron. Astrophys.*, **399**, 703

O'Donnell, J.E. (1994) *Astrophys. J.*, **422**, 158

Onaka, T. (1980) *Ann. Tokyo Astron. Obs.*, **18**, 1

Oort, J.H. and van de Hulst, H.C. (1946) *Bull. Astron. Inst. Netherlandes*, **10**, 187

Ossenkopf, V. (1991) *Astron. Astrophys.*, **251**, 210

Ossenkopf, V., Henning, Th. and Mathis, J.S. (1992) *Astron. Astrophys.*, **261**, 567

Palik, E.D. (1998) In *Handbook of Optical Constants of Solids III*, ed. by E.D. Palik, Academic Press, New York, p. 507

Parenago, P.P. (1940) *Astron. Zh.*, **17**, 3

Patriarchi, P., Morbidelli, L. and Perinotti, M. (2003) *Astron. Astrophys.*, **410**, 905

Perelman, A.Y. (1979) *Appl. Optics* **18**, 2307

Perelman, A.Y. and Voshchinnikov, N.V. (2002a) *J. Quant. Spectrosc. Rad. Transfer*, **72**, 607

Perelman, A.Y. and Voshchinnikov, N.V. (2002b) *Optics Spectrosc.*, **92**, 221

Petrov, Yu.A. (1986) *Clusters and Small Particles*, Nauka, Moscow

Philipp, H.R. (1985) In *Handbook of Optical Constants of Solids* ed. by E.D. Palik, Academic Press, New York, p. 719

Pier, E.A. and Krolik, J.H. (1992) *Astrophys. J.*, **401**, 99

Popowski, P., Cook, K.H. and Becker, A.C. (2003) *Astron. J.*, **126**, 2910

Prishivalko, A.P., Babenko, V.A. and Kuz'min, V.N. (1984) *Scattering and Absorption of Light by Inhomogeneous and Anisotropic Spherical Particles*, Nauka i Tekhnika, Minsk

Purcell, E. M. (1979) *Astrophys. J.*, **231**, 404

Purcell, E. M. and Pennypacker, C.R. (1973) *Astrophys. J.*, **186**, 705

Lord Rayleigh (1881) *Philos. Mag.*, **12**, 81

Rieke, G.H. and Lebofsky, M.J. (1985) *Astrophys. J.*, **288**, 618

Roberge, W.G. (1996) In *Polarimetry of the Interstellar Medium*, ed. by W.G. Roberge and D.C.B. Whittet, ASP Conf. Ser., **97**, p. 401

Roessler, D.M. and Huffman, D.R. (1991) In *Handbook of Optical Constants of Solids II* ed. by E.D. Palik, Academic Press, New York, p. 949

Rogers, C. and Martin, P.G. (1979) *Astrophys. J.*, **228**, 450

Rogers, C. and Martin, P.G. (1986) *Astrophys. J.*, **311**, 800

Rouleau, F. and Martin, P.G. (1991) *Astrophys. J.*, **377**, 526

Rouleau, F., Henning, Th. and Stognienko, R. (1997) *Astron. Astrophys.*, **322**, 633

Rowan-Robinson, M. (1980) *Astrophys. J. Suppl.*, **44**, 403

Ryter, Ch.E. (1996) *Astrophys. Space Sci.*, **236**, 285

Sasseen, T.P., Hurwitz, M., Dixon, W.V. and Airieau, S. (2002) *Astrophys. J.*, **566**, 267

Savage, B.D. and Mathis, J.S. (1979) *Annu. Rev. Astron. Astrophys.*, **17**, 73

Savage, B.D. and Sembach, K.R. (1996) *Annu. Rev. Astron. Astrophys.*, **34**, 279

Schalén, C. (1933) *Medd. Astron. Observ. Upsala*, **58**

Schalén, C. (1936) *Medd. Astron. Observ. Upsala*, **64**

Schlegel, D.J., Finkbeiner, D.P. and Davies, M. (1998) *Astrophys. J.*, **500**, 525

Schnaiter, M., Mutschke, H., Dorschner, J., Henning, Th. and Salama, F. (1998) *Astrophys. J.*, **498**, 486

Schoenberg, E. and Jung, B. (1934) *Astron. Nachr.*, **253**, 261

Schuerman, D.W. (1980) In *Light Scattering by Irregularly Shaped Particles*, ed. by D.W. Schuerman, Plenum, New York, p. 227

Schultheis, M., Ganesh, S., Simon, G., Omont, A., Alard, C., Borsenberger, J., Copet, E., Epchtein, N., Fouqué, P. and Habing, H. (1999) *Astron. Astrophys.*, **349**, L69

Schulz, N.S., Cui, W., Canizares, C.R., Marshall, H.L., Lee, J.C., Miller, J.M. and Lewin, W.H.G. (2002) *Astrophys. J.*, **565**, 1141

Seaton, M.J. (1979) *Monthly Notices RAS*, **187**, 73P

Serkowski, K. (1973) In *Interstellar Dust and Related Topics*, ed. by J.M. Greenberg and D.S. Hayes, IAU Symp., **52**, p. 145

Serkowski, K., Mathewson, D.S. and Ford, V.L. (1975) *Astrophys. J.*, **196**, 261

Shah, G. (1970) *Monthly Notices RAS*, **148**, 93

Shah, G. (1992) *Astrophys. Space Sci.*, **193**, 317

Shapiro, P.R. (1975) *Astrophys. J.*, **201**, 151

Sharpless, S. (1963) *Interstellar Reddening*, In *Basic Astronomical Data*, ed. by K. Strand, Chicago Univ. Press, Chicago, p. 225

Shifrin, K.S. (1951) *Scattering of Light in a Turbid Medium*, Gostekhizdat, Moscow-Leningrad

Shifrin, K.S. (1952) *Izvestia Academii Nauk SSSR, Ser. Geofizicheskaya*, N 2, 15

Sihvola, A.H. (1989) *IEEE Trans. on Geoscience and Remote Sensing*, **27**, 403

Sihvola, A.H. (1999) *Electromagnetic Mixing Formulas and Applications*, Institute of Electrical Engineers, Electromagnetic Waves Series 47, London

Skórzyński, W., Strobel, A. and Galazutdinov, G.A. (2003) *Astron. Astrophys.*, **408**, 297

Snow, T.P. (2000) *J. Geophys. Res.*, **105**, 10239

Snow, T.P. and Witt, A.N. (1995) *Science*, **270**, 1455

Snow, T.P. and Witt, A.N. (1996) *Astrophys. J.*, **468**, L65

Snow, T.P., Allen, M.M. and Polidan, R.S. (1990) *Astrophys. J.*, **359**, L23

Sobolev, V.V. (1975) *Light Scattering in Planetary Atmospheres*, Pergamon Press, Oxford

Sofia, U.J. and Meyer, D.M. (2001) *Astrophys. J.*, **554**, L221 [Erratum: **558**, L147]

Sonnhalter, C., Preibisch, Th. and York, H.W. (1995) *Astron. Astrophys.*, **299**, 545

Sorrell, W.H. (1990) *Monthly Notices RAS*, **243**, 570

Spagna, G.F. and Leung, C.M. (1983) *Computer Physics Comm.*, **28**, 337

Spagna, G.F. and Leung, C.M. (1987) *J. Quant. Spectrosc. Rad. Transfer*, **37**, 565

Spanier, J.E. and Herman, I.P. (2000) *Phys. Rev.*, **B61**, 10437

Stamatellos, D. and Whitworth, A.P. (2003) *Astron. Astrophys.*, **407**, 941

Stecher, T.P. (1965) *Astrophys. J.*, **142**, 1683

Stecher, T.P. and Donn, B. (1965) *Astrophys. J.*, **142**, 1681

Steele, I.A., Negueruela, I., Coe, M.J. and Roche, P. (1998) *Monthly Notices RAS*, **297**, L5

Steinacker, J., Henning, Th., Bacmann, A. and Semenov, D. (2003) *Astron. Astrophys.*, **401**, 405

Stognienko, R., Henning, Th. and Ossenkopf, V. (1995) *Astron. Astrophys.*, **296**, 797

Straižys, V. (1978) *Bull. Vinius Obs.*, N 47, 27

Straižys, V. (1992) *Multicolor Stellar Photometry*, Pachart Publ. House, Tucson

Sumi, T. (2003) *astro-ph*/0300206

Takei, Y., Fujimoto, R., Mitsuda, K. and Onaka, T. (2002) *Astrophys. J.*, **581**, 307

Teixeira, T.C., and Emerson, J.P. (1999) *Astron. Astrophys.*, **351**, 303

Tikhov, G. (1910) *Trans. Russian Astron. Soc.*, **10**, 1 and 90

Tinbergen, J. (1996) *Astronomical Polarimetry*, Cambridge University Press

Trumpler, R.J. (1930) *Lick Observ. Bull.*, **14**, 154

Tsang, L., Kong, J.A. and Shin, R.T. (1985) *Theory of Microwave Remote Sensing*, John Wiley, New York

Udalski, A. (2003) *Astrophys. J.*, **590**, 284

Ueta, T. and Meixner, M. (2003) *Astrophys. J.*, **586**, 1338

Vaidya, D.B., Gupta, R., Dobbie, J.S. and Chýlek, P. (2001) *Astron. Astrophys.*, **375**, 584

van Bemmel, I.M. and Dullemond, C.P. (2003) *Astron. Astrophys.*, **404**, 1

van de Hulst, H.C. (1949) *Rech. Astron. Observ. Utrecht* **11**, Part 2

van de Hulst, H.C. (1957) *Light Scattering by Small Particles*, John Wiley, New York

Városi, F. and Dwek, E. (1999) *Astrophys. J.*, **523**, 265

Videen, G. and Chýlek, P. (1998) *Optics Comm.*, **158**, 1

Videen, G., Fu, Q. and Chýlek, P. (ed.) (2001) *J. Quant. Spectrosc. Rad. Transfer*, **70**, N 4-6

Volten, H. (2001) *PhD Thesis*, Free University, Amsterdam

Voshchinnikov, N.V. (1989) *Astron. Nachr.*, **310**, 265

Voshchinnikov, N.V. (1990) *Sov. Astron.*, **34**, 535

Voshchinnikov, N.V. (1996) *J. Quant. Spectrosc. Rad. Transfer*, **55**, 627

Voshchinnikov, N.V. (2001) In *IRS 2000: Current Problems in Atmospheric Radiation*, ed. by W.L. Smith and Yu.M. Timofeyev, A. Deepak Publ., p. 237

Voshchinnikov, N.V. and Farafonov, V.G. (1985) *Optics Spectrosc.*, **58**, 81

Voshchinnikov, N.V. and Farafonov, V.G. (1993) *Astrophys. Space Sci.*, **204**, 19

Voshchinnikov, N.V. and Farafonov, V.G. (2000) *Optics Spectrosc.*, **88**, 78

Voshchinnikov, N.V. and Farafonov, V.G. (2002) *Measurement Sci. and Technology*, **13**, 249

Voshchinnikov, N.V. and Il'in, V.B. (1987) *Sov. Astron. Lett.*, **13**, 157

Voshchinnikov, N.V. and Il'in, V.B. (1993) *Astron. Rep.*, **37**, 21

Voshchinnikov, N.V. and Karjukin, V.V. (1994) *Astron. Astrophys.*, **288**, 883

Voshchinnikov, N.V. and Mathis, J.S. (1999) *Astrophys. J.*, **526**, 257

Voshchinnikov, N.V., Il'in, A.E. and Il'in, V.B. (1986) *Astrophysics*, **24**, 299

Voshchinnikov, N.V., Il'in, V.B., Henning, Th., Michel, B. and Farafonov, V.G. (2000) *J. Quant. Spectrosc. Rad. Transfer*, **65**, 877

Voshchinnikov, N.V., Il'in, V.B., Henning, Th. and Dubkova, D.N. (2003) *Astron. Astrophys.*, in preparation

Vuong, M.H., Montmerle, T., Grosso, N., Feigelson, E.D., Verstraete, L. and Ozawa, H. (2003) *Astron. Astrophys.*, **408**, 581

Wait, J.R. (1955) *Can. J. Phys.*, **33**, 189

Wait, J.R. (1963) *Appl. Sci. Res. Sect.*, **33**, 189

Warren, S.G. (1984) *Appl. Optics*, **23**, 1206

Warren-Smith, R.F. (1983) *Monthly Notices RAS*, **205**, 337

Waterman, P.C. (1971) *Phys. Rev.*, **3D**, 825

Waxman, E. and Draine, B.T. (2000) *Astrophys. J.*, **537**, 796

Weingartner, J.C. and Draine, B.T. (2001) *Astrophys. J.*, **548**, 296

Weingartner, J.C. and Draine, B.T. (2003) *Astrophys. J.*, **589**, 289

Wegner, W. (2003) *Astron. Nachr.*, **324**, 219

White, R.L. (1979) *Astrophys. J.*, **230**, 116

Whitney, B.A. and Hartmann, L. (1992) *Astrophys. J.*, **395**, 529

Whitney, B.A. and Wolff, M.J. (2002) *Astrophys. J.*, **574**, 205

Whittet, D.C.B. (1992) *Dust in the Galactic Environments*, Institute of Physics Publishing, New York

Whittet, D.C.B. (1996a) In *The Cosmic Dust Connection*, ed. by J.M. Greenberg, Kluwer, p. 155

Whittet, D.C.B. (1996b) In *Polarimetry of the Interstellar Medium*, ed. by W.G. Roberge and D.C.B. Whittet, ASP Conf. Ser., **97**, p. 125

Whittet, D.C.B. (2003) *Dust in the Galactic Environments*, Second Edition, Institute of Physics Publishing, Bristol

Whittet, D.C.B. and van Breda, I.G. (1978) *Astron. Astrophys.*, **66**, 57

Whittet, D.C.B., Kirrane, T.M., Kilkeny, D. Oates, A.P., Watson, F.G. and King, D.J. (1987) *Monthly Notices RAS*, **224**, 497

Whittet, D.C.B., Martin, P.G., Hough, J.H., Rouse, M.F., Bailey, J.A. and Axon, D.J. (1992) *Astrophys. J.*, **386**, 562

Wickramasinghe, N.C. (1963) *Monthly Notices RAS*, **126**, 99
Wickramasinghe, N.C. and Guillaume, C. (1965) *Nature*, **207**, 366
Wiener, O. (1910) *Berichte über die Verhandlungen der Königlich-Sächsischen Gesellschaft der Wisseschaften zu Leipzig, Math.-phys. Klasse*, **62**, 256
Wilking, B.A., Lebofsky, M.J. and Rieke, G.H. (1982) *Astron. J.*, **87**, 695
Wilms, J., Allen, A. and McCray, R. (2000) *Astrophys. J.*, **542**, 914
Wiscombe, W.J. (1980) *Appl. Optics*, **19**, 1505
Witt, A.N. (1977) *Astrophys. J. Suppl.*, **35**, 1
Wolf, S. (2003) *Computer Physics Comm.*, **150**, 99
Wolf, S. and Henning, Th. (2000) *Computer Physics Comm.*, **132**, 166
Wolf, S. and Voshchinnikov, N.V. (2004) *Computer Physics Comm.*, in press
Wolf, S., Voshchinnikov, N.V. and Henning, Th. (2002) *Astron. Astrophys.*, **385**, 365
Wolff, M.J., Clayton, G.C. and Gibson, S.J. (1998) *Astrophys. J.*, **503**, 815
Wolff, M.J., Clayton, G.C. and Meade, M.R. (1993) *Astrophys. J.*, **403**, 722
Wolff, M.J., Clayton, G.C., Martin, P.G. and Schulte-Ladbeck, R.E. (1994) *Astrophys. J.*, **423**, 412
Wolfire, M.G. and Cassinelli, J.P. (1986) *Astrophys. J.*, **310**, 207
Woolf, N.J. and Ney, E.P. (1969) *Astrophys. J.*, **155**, L181
Wriedt, T. (1998) *Part. Part. Syst. Charact.*, **15**, 67
Wriedt, T. and Comberg, U. (1998) *J. Quant. Spectrosc. Radiat. Transfer*, **60**, 425
Wright, E.L. (1998) *Astrophys. J.*, **496**, 1
Wurm, G. and Schnaiter, M. (2002) *Astrophys. J.*, **567**, 370
Wu, Z.S. and Wang, Y.P. (1991) *Radio Sci.*, **26**, 1393
Yeh, C. and Lindgren, G. (1977) *Appl. Optics*, **16**, 483
Yorke, H.W. (1980) *Astron. Astrophys.*, **86**, 286
Zakharova, N.T. and Mishchenko, M.I. (2000) *Appl. Optics*, **39**, 5052
Zerull, R. and Giese, R.H. (1974) In *Planets, Stars, and Nebulae Studied with Photopolarimetry*, ed. by T. Gehrels, Tucson, Univ. Arizona Press, p. 901
Zubko, V.G., Dwek, E. and Arendt, G. (2003) *astro-ph/0312641*
Zubko, V.G., Krełowski, J. and Wegner, W. (1996) *Monthly Notices RAS*, **283**, 577
Zubko, V.G., Krełowski, J. and Wegner, W. (1998) *Monthly Notices RAS*, **294**, 548

INDEX

ASTROPHYSICS AND SPACE PHYSICS REVIEWS

Editor: R.A. Sunyaev
Institute for Space Research
Russian Academy of Sciences
Moscow, Russia

Advisory Editor: M. Longair
Cavendish Laboratory
University of Cambridge
UK

GENERAL INFORMATION

Aims and Scope

Astrophysics and Space Physics Reviews publishes review articles covering significant developments in astronomy, theoretical astrophysics, cosmology, high energy astrophysics and space research in the former Soviet Union. Plans for future space experiments are also highlighted.

Ordering Information

Each volume consists of an irregular number of parts depending upon extent. Issues are available individually as well as by subscription. 2003/2004 Volume 12/13.

Orders may be placed with your usual supplier or at the address shown below. Journal subscriptions are sold on a per volume basis only. Claims for nonreceipt of issues will be honored if made within three months of publication of the issue. All issues are dispatched by airmail throughout the world.

Subscription Rates

Base list subscription price per volume: EUR 120.00. * This price is available only to individuals whose library subscribes to the journal OR who warrant that the journal is for their own use and provide a home address for mailing. Orders must be sent directly to the Publisher and payment must be made by personal check or credit card. Separate rates apply to academic and corporate/government institutions.

*EUR (Euro). The Euro is the worldwide base list currency rate. All other currency payments should be made using the current conversion rate set by the Publisher. Subscribers should contact their agents or the Publisher. All prices are subject to change without notice.

Orders should be placed through the Publisher at the following addresses:

Cambridge Scientific Publishers
P.O. Box 806
Cottenham
Cambridge
CB4 8RT
UK
Tel: +44 (0)1954 251283
Fax: +44 (0)1954 252517
Email: janie.wardle@cambridgescientificpublishers.com
Website: www.cambridgescientificpublishers.com

Printed in UK

April 2004

Printed in the United Kingdom
by Lightning Source UK Ltd.
101304UKS00001B/154-189